Kaleidoscope:
Life's Meaningful Reflections

Volume Three

There's Greatness Within You!!!

Vanessa Conaway Pace

Pace Publishing International
Post Office Box 2187
Lynnwood, WA 98036

www.pacepublishing.com

Kaleidoscope: Life's Meaningful Reflections
Volume Three: There's Greatness Within You!!!

Prose, Poetry, Music, and Design Created By:

Vanessa Conaway Pace

Cover Design by: milagraphicartist@gmail.com

ISBN Number: ISBN-13: 978-0-9704373-2-7

ISBN-10: 0-9704373-2-3

Copyright © 2018 by: Pace Publishing
Post Office Box 2187
Lynnwood, WA 98036 USA

www.pacepublishing.com

Printed/Duplicated in the United States of America. All rights to this book and its design are reserved to the Author under International Copyright Law. No part of this design, these contents and/or cover may be reproduced in whole or in part in any form by any means—electronic, mechanical, photocopy, video or audio recording, or any other—except for brief quotations in printed reviews, without the prior express written consent of the Publisher.

About The Author

Vanessa Conaway Pace is a direct descendant of the Welsh Bards, and is an Award-Winning Poet, "with the distinction of Poet Fellow, in honor of creative work", by Nobel House, London, England, 2007. (See pages 97 and 179.) This current Volume is the **third** in the **"Kaleidoscope"** Books and Audio Series of **"Life's Meaningful Reflections"**.

She is an international singer with 9 albums (in 5 languages) to her credit, is Host and Producer of two long-running weekly half-hour television series, along with numerous television specials, and is a frequent presenter at conferences and seminars.

Vanessa is creator of the voice training books and audio series entitled "Managing Your Computerized Voice Box", and is Co-Author of "For The Love Of Children: A Guidebook for Early Childhood Education".

As a Teacher of the Creative Arts, Vanessa Coaches Voice in her Studio in Lynnwood, WA, and internationally via electronic media. She holds a Bachelor of Arts Degree in Music Performance, and maintains a varied performing career ranging from Opera to Broadway.

> "My Life's Kaleidoscope is ever-changing: ...: Writing, Singing, Teaching, Coaching, Creating, Concertizing, Producing books/greeting cards/albums, ...,
>
> "..., Learning/Researching/Lecturing about The Power of Sound and the scientific and esoteric basis thereof, ...,
>
> "What a wonderful world we have to explore, and understand, and subdue!"
> Vanessa

Other Books and Materials By This Author

Also in the **"Kaleidoscope"** Series: "Kaleidoscope: Life's Meaningful Reflections" Volume 1: "That's ENUF!!!"; Volume 2: "One Great Gift"

"For The Love Of Children: A Guidebook for Early Childhood Education";
with Marguerite Laskares and Tamra Pace

"Secrets of Voice Development for Speakers and Singers" Course Numbers 1 and 2

"Rejoice! A Celebration of Christmas" Music Cd

"He's Alive!!!": Gospel Music Cd, Sung in English

"El E Viu": Gospel Music Cd, Sung in Romanian

"Yazutse!!!": Gospel Music Cd, Sung in Kenyarwandan (the native language of Rwanda)

"The Master's Voice": Hymns in Classical Settings, Sung in English

"Lodiamo Dio": Hymns in Classical Settings, Sung in Italian

"Din Dragostea": "To Romania With Love", Hymns in Classical Settings, Sung in Romanian

"Great Classical Arias and Duets":
with Finnish Coloratura Mezzo Soprano
Helena Niemispelto;
Sung in English, Italian, Finnish, and Latin

www.pacepublishing.com

Dedication

*To Mother and Daddy,
Freeda and George Conaway,
who gave me a love for words,
and their meaning,
and their power,
and their expressive beauty.*

*Thanks for all those hours
when you read to me,
and encouraged me,
and helped me
to Be Who I AM!*

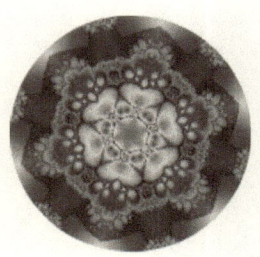

www.pacepublishing.com

Acknowledgements

M y dear friend, ...,
    a remarkable Healer, Intuitive,
        life-long student of the human body,
            its mechanisms,
        and the natural, logical repair thereof,

    had sent me a package containing a sheath of
    fascinating explanations for the underlying causes
        of human dis-ease and suffering,
            and their natural cures.

Armed with that,
        and my ever-present teapot, honey,
            and favorite Angel China mug,
            I retreated to the back yard
        to bask in the all-too-rare Seattle sunlight!

        Ah! The breath of the warm air,
            the song of the birds,
                and the ever present roar
            of the interstate I-5 traffic in my ears!
I hear the traffic's incessant sound
        as a magnificent giant waterfall.

I sense the fine spray on my face,
        and "see" its vaporous rainbows
            as the water tumbles into the pools below.

            Life is peaceful!!

The articles in my precious package contain life-giving information for humans suffering physical pains, and often there is a testimony of someone's remarkable healing and recovery when using the information that was shared by its author. Always there was the profuse expression of profound gratitude to those unselfish ones who had shared the precious information.

I remembered others who had unselfishly shared the priceless truths of their experience and study: ...:

- The folks at The Farm; and warm nights and days of exciting sharings about what we were learning;

- The invaluable teaching from my Beloved Maestro, who guided my Voice into its full potential of magnificent sound that would comfort, bless, excite, and heal, audiences around the world;

- My Mother and Father's constant, and endless, impartations of instructions, wisdom, and loving correction;

- My Friend's encouragement and insightful inputs as we write our books and journey through life;

- My computer guru's patient explanations of how that little beastie works, so that I can create books, record my own music and poetry, create videos and my television programs, research the ever-unfolding story of Creation, and communicate with the outside world;

- *The esoteric and true scientific writings of the Ancients (and some Moderns) who freely offered their treasures to any interested takers.*

On and on the list goes. To these unselfish sharers goes my unending gratitude. They are all a part of what I am today, and will surely share richly in the joys and rewards I receive for the faithful completion of my contract for this visit to Planet Earth.

Maybe it isn't just "Love" that makes the world go round. Maybe it is more correct to say that it is the many random acts of kindness, and the tireless dissemination of Truths, and Wisdom, and exciting revelations of our unseen friends, the authors, who have provided/created the energy to make it all go round! We are all so grateful for your faithfulness to develop and share your particular gifts and talents. Your contribution to our (and society's) growth and development raises the frequency of our collective consciousness exponentially!. You set us a fine example of how exciting our own life can be when we share our joys and expertise with others, ...,

..., Hmmm! What's this? ...? I feel a poem coming on, ...,

www.pacepublishing.com

We Share

We share
      What We know
           And so
                  We all grow
                        Into Awesome Light Beings
                          Of Power.

We earn
      What We learn
           And then We
                In our turn
                      Pass it on
                          So that others
                              Can flower.

It's no fun
      When you play
           By yourself,
                All alone,
                      With the subjects
                          That make you
                              So happy.

It's when **you**
      Share it
           With others
                Of your sisters
                      And brothers
                          That your life
                              Becomes fulfilled
                                  And snappy!!

When your knowledge
    Is kept
        In some dark
            Stagnant pool
                You'll feel bloated
                    And stuck
                        In your ways;

But when it flows
    Like a river,
        And You
            Are the giver,
                You'll find Joy
                    And delight
                        In your days.

Never mind
    That you're churning
        For more facts
            And more learning;

Take a break
    From your sponge-like mentality. ...,

    Look around.
        There's a dearth
            Of your knowledge
                On Earth;
                    And your sharing
                      Brings you back
                        To Reality!!

Its not fair
    When you know it
        And keep it
            To Self,
                When the others
                    Are starving
                        Without it.

Give it air!
    Give it wings!
        Then your Soul
            Really Sings.
                The results
                    Leave you
                        No room
                            To doubt it!

So, Whatever your interest,
    Or your Soul's
        Inclination,
            Better heed it,
                And give yourself
                    To it;

And then,
    Follow that up
        As you fill up your cup
            With the Sharing
                That helps
                    Us all
                        Do it!!!!!

                        Vanessa Conaway Pace
                Lynnwood, Washington, May 3, 2013

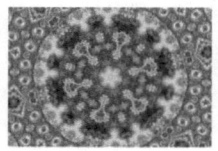

My deep gratitude also goes to my friend and colleague,
Marguerite Laskares, who has taken time from her own
brilliant work in Early Childhood Education*,
to provide invaluable editorial and production assistance
on this Volume.

Many thanks for all those happy creative hours!!!

*See "For The Love Of Children: A Guidebook For Early Childhood",
Marguerite Laskares at Amazon.com.

Table of Contents

Frontispieces

About the Author	3
Other Books and Publications by the Author	4
Dedication	5
Acknowledgements: "My dear friend," …,	7
Poem: "We Share"	11
Table of Contents	15
Prologue: Dear Seeker of those "deeper things"	19
Foreword: "There ARE No Limitations"	21
Epigraphs: "Kaleidoscope", …, "cre-ate"	25
Introduction: "In E-ve-ry Moment".	29

Reflections

Fireworks!!!	35
Inspirational Background	37
Poem	45
Reader's Reflections	53
FOCUS	59
Inspirational Background	61
Poem	69
Reader's Reflections	73
The Crys-tal-line Sea	79
Inspirational Background	81
Poem	91
Reader's Reflections	97
Ill-lumen-a-ti	103
Inspirational Background	105
Poem	111
Reader's Reflections	119

In A Parallel Universe	*125*
Inspirational Background	*127*
Poem	*131*
Reader's Reflections	*133*
Its The Energy You Send Out	*139*
Inspirational Background	*141*
Poem	*147*
Reader's Reflections	*155*
No Meaning???	*161*
Inspirational Background	*163*
Poem	*173*
Reader's Reflections	*175*
Our Purpose	*181*
Inspirational Background	*183*
Poem	*191*
Reader's Reflections	*199*
The High Road	*205*
Inspirational Background	*207*
Poem	*213*
Song	*217*
Reader's Reflections	*227*
The Flow of Love	*233*
Inspirational Background	*235*
Poem	*243*
Reader's Reflections	*249*
There's Greatness Within You!!!	*255*
Inspirational Background	*257*
Poem	*261*
Reader's Reflections	*265*

Epilogue	*271*
Poem: "Now that We've finished":	*273*
Reader's Reflections	*279*
Reading List	*285*

www.pacepublishing.com

Prologue

Dear Seeker of those "deeper things",

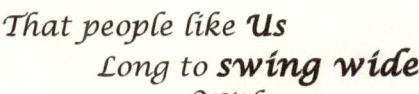

This poetry's written
    From **My** heart
        To **Yours**,
            To help Us **unlock**
                All those Creative doors

That people like **Us**
    Long to **swing wide**
        With ease, ...,
           But we fear
              Catching cold
                  In that Creative breeze

That fans
    Our Great Love
        Of Creating things, ...,
            And then knowing
                The Joys that
                    All of that brings.

So, **"FOCUS"** in now,
    For just a minute,
        And find the **Joy** of **LIFE**
            That's in it
                When **Us LIKE people**
                Pause to sit,
                    And **let** Ourselves
                      Just dream
                        A bit.
                  Vanessa

www.pacepublishing.com

Foreword

There ARE No Limitations

"*There ARE*
    No Limitations"
        To the Life
            That **You** have planned,

Except the ones
    That **You** create,
        Which really
            Should be banned!

There **IS**
    No force
        That's out there
            Saying "Stop him
                From the start".

Oh, NO!
    THE Force
        That starts and stops
            Is deep within
                Your heart!

So, **let** Its message Bubble up, ...,
    Then grab Your ink and pen
        And start to write
            "The Plan", and then,
                Just let the work
                    BEGIN!!!

The **Truth** is
    That **We cannot fail**
        If we will
            Just take action; ...;
                So, **step right out**
                    And realize
                        A life of satisfaction.

It's getting that belief
    Inside
        So our **subconscious** rules...
            Because Our well-trained Mind's
                Equipped
                    With "**Tools**
                      That Don't Make
                          Fools"!!

We cease to **do**
    The things that **We**
        Don't want to do
            In life, ...,
    And then begin
        To gauge our step
            To a higher-sounding fife,

Where **Our Mission**
    And Our Purpose
        Manifest
            With quiet ease,
                And We discover
                    Being Masters
                    Really **IS**
                        A breeze!

You are capable
  Of greatness,
    *And **Destined** to it, too;*
      So, the smartest thing
        That you can do
          *Is **grab yourself***
            A clue!

You've had it stored
  For all these years
    Of quiet desperation,
      *And **now's** the time*
        To bring it through
          With work,
            And perspiration.

*Just **"FOCUS" in***
  On what has always
    Brought You
      *Lots of **Joy**, ...,*
        *And then, **Pursue it***
          Day and night,
            Like kids enjoy
              A toy!

You'll find Your vision
  Taking shape.
    The more you take some action;
      So, don Your Cape,
        *You **"Superman"**,*
          And fly
            Without distraction.

And soon You'll live
>A greater life
>>Of **PURPOSE, GAIN,**
>>>And **TRACTION,**
>>>>With every moment **counting**
>>>>Toward Your work
>>>>>Of **satisfaction**.

And ***all*** will know
>You came down here
>>To make Your mark below, ...,
>>>In this frequency
>>>>That's lower than
>>>>>The one that makes
>>>>>>**You** glow!

You've got the tools
>Built right inside, ...,
>>Stored there
>>>For your convenience;
>>>>So, dust them off,
>>>>>And then apply them
>>>>>>To Your task
>>>>>>>With lenience.

And soon
>You'll go 'round **humming**
>>**Happy tunes**
>>>**That spark Your day,**
>>>>And set the Fires Of Life **Ablaze,**
>>>>And get **You**
>>>>>**Making hay!!!**

Vanessa Conaway Pace
Lynnwood, Washington, January 29, 2016

Epigraphs

"**Kaleidoscope,** n. 1. *an optical tube in which bits of glass and beads are shown in changing symmetrical forms by reflection in two or more mirrors as the tube is turned.*
2. anything that shifts continually."
The Random House Dictionary,
Ballentine Books, New York

"**Kaleidoscope** ,   ...; *picturesquely diversified.*"
The Practical Standard Dictionary
of the English Language,
Funk & Wagnalls Company,
New York, 1928

That's US!!!

www.pacepublishing.com

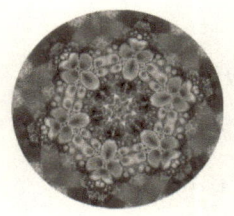

"cre-ate´, ..., 1. To cause to come into existence; especially, to produce out of nothing. 2. To produce as a new construction out of existing materials."

The Practical Standard Dictionary;
Funk & Wagnalls Company,
New York, 1928

Oh, I feel a poem coming on!!! ....

"cre-a´tion, ..., 1. The act of creating;
    production without use of preexistent material;
        ...; 2. An act of construction,
            physical or mental;
                the combining or organizing
                    of existing materials
                        into new form; ...."

The Practical Standard Dictionary;
Funk & Wagnalls Company,
New York, 1928

Oh!!! That describes US as the individual pieces of The Great Kaleidoscope of Life!!!

Oh, I do, indeed, feel *poems* coming on!!!

Introduction
In E-ve-ry Moment

"**In E-ve-ry Moment**"
    You **should**
        Understand
            Something new
                In your personal
                    Land.

Let something **NEW**
    Flow into
        Your **Mind,**
            And then
                Feed the process
                    By which
                        Its refined.

For mental stagnation
    Will be Your
        Nemesis,
            So, bring some
                NEW stuff
                    Into Your
                        Premises!

Learn
    How the Earth works,
        And **why**
            Water flows;
                Examine
                    The "**Creation**"
                      That's under
                          Your nose.

Observe
>*Why* a plant grows,
>>Or,
>>>*How* a bird flies; ...;
>>>*Look* at the
>>>>"*Wonders*"
>>>>>Under Our skies;

Question
>*Who* made You,
>>And *how*
>>>You got *here*, ...,
>>>>And *how*
>>>>>All those *Sound waves*
>>>>>>Got into
>>>>>>>Your ear.

Just *wonder*
>How *everything*
>>Came into Being; ...;
>>>And *what* made
>>>>Those *beauteous*
>>>>>*Colors*
>>>>>>You're seeing.

Explore
>Things in *Nature*, ...,
>>And *what*
>>>Makes *You tick*; ...;
>>>>And then,
>>>>>While You're at it,
>>>>>>*Explain*
>>>>>>>Why You're
>>>>>>>>*Sick!*

When **All**
    Was **created**
        From **Light**,
            In the First place,
                Then **why**
                    Is it functioning **Weird**
                        In this **New** space?

"In E-ve-ry Moment"
    You'll **learn**
        Something **NEW**,
            If you'll **ask**
                The right questions,
                And then,
                    You'll **review**!

Yes!
    Life can be Beautiful
        If You'll get **out** of Your rut, ...,
            And **put forth**
                The effort
                    To get off of
                        Your... Back side, ...,

And venture
    Outside
        Of the boundaries
            You've **LET**
                Be established
                    By somebody **else's**
                        Strong net

That has **held You**
>For eons,
>>And eons of time; ...;
>>>But, the "Time"
>>>>Has now come
>>>>>To find out
>>>>**You're Sublime!!!**

With all of the
>**Qualities**
>>You've drawn
>>>From **Source**, ...
>>>>..., Including Divinity, ...,
>>>>**Its Your Birthright,**
>>>>>Of course!!!

So, **begin**
>**To seek out**
>>Who **You**
>>>Really ***ARE***,
>>>>And then, **walk**
>>>>>In that knowledge, ...,
>>>>>>..., It will take You
>>>>>>>Quite far,

And You'll **never be bored**,
>Or **depressed**,
>>Or **fatigued**; ...;
>>>..., How could You be **When**
>>>>You are ***FULLY*** Intrigued

With the **beauties**
>   Around You, ...,
>   And the **potentials**
>   Within, ...,
>   Oh, just **think**
>   About **all**
>   We've been given,
>   And then

Share Your stuff,
>   Like The **Poet** has done
>   In this book, ...,
>   And **encourage**
>   Some others
>   To take
>   A **new** look

At the **Infinite Life**
>   That We're all
>   **Swimming in;** ...;
>   ...; **Then**
>   We'll **all**
>   Join the Song; ...;

Let the Journey Begin!!!

> > > Vanessa Conaway Pace
> > > Lynnwood, Washington, February 7, 2016

www.pacepublishing.com

Fireworks!!!

www.pacepublishing.com

Fireworks!!!
Inspirational Background

We were living in Boston, and life had taken a turn for what I perceived was "the worst". One thing about "hard times" is that the survival instinct in us kicks in, and begins to call in the answers we need, while the lesser parts of us go about the pre-programmed "victim's path of least resistance". We cry, we moan, we complain, we seek sympathy by telling our sad stories over and over to anyone who will listen, and we blame others for our plight. Its only later that we realize it was all wasted energy, and, we floundered because of the pain, and because of the loss of "direction" and "drive". The wind has been knocked out of our sails, and we just "hurt", and "fear" this ominous interruption to our lives. It would be easy to quit.

But, the good news is that in times like these we also begin to question, "Where am I going? What am I supposed to be doing? What is life all about?" And, my own all-time quest, ..., "What makes these things tick?" In the words of the old popular song, "What's It All About, Alfie?"

But we live in a most exciting era! The energies of the Universe are bombarding our home planet with delicious Truths that our sleeping populace has long since forgotten, but shall surely need again as we collectively walk through this current experience of growing, and ascending, and learning those new and exciting Truths, and how to apply them.

Many are the times that we feel alone, and long for another fellow traveler from whom we can learn new Truths, and with whom we can share our newly remembered awakenings to the magnificent workings of The Master Plan of Creation.

When we begin to **ask** the important questions, our seekings will inevitably bring us some answers. And then our gregarious personality naturally wants to talk with others about the answers that our seekings have brought us. But oftentimes we find that we have walked out of the old familiar world in which we were comfortable, and into a lonely, vast wasteland, with no one to share our exuberance about our new-found Truths. We long for others to enlighten us more, and understanding ears to share the joys of our new discoveries, only to find that our exuberance brings yawns of disinterest, or, worse yet, because they have not walked in those hallowed halls in which we have trod, outright rejection and ridicule that brings even more pain.

However, there are those who have paid an awesome price to uncover the buried treasures of Truth, and who have been faithful to write, record, and video the results of their labors so that others can share their hard-earned insights and experiences. To those Authors, Producers, and Keepers of the Libraries (often unsung) civilization owes a deep debt of gratitude.

My search for others of the flesh and blood kind who would sit and talk with me, and who could confirm that the post-graduate things that I was coming to understand on my own were actually True came up with a big "Zero". Was there nobody in the whole metropolis who understood, and was willing to talk about, the world that my eyes had been opened to?

I would not be left comfortless! Books had been my "Friends" from my earliest days, when Mother and Daddy spent endless hours reading to me, making the characters come alive, pointing out the morals of the stories, and musically dancing through the vast poetry library with inflections in their voices that captivated my little ears, and sent the rhyming rhythms pulsating through my very bones. I knew the **feelings** of words. I felt the mesmerizing beat, and the rise and fall of their flow.

I had often sought solace in the words of my **unseen** "Friends". I knew how to look for answers on the printed page. The more I sought answers, the more precious books began coming my way. I found my mentors!

Authors have always been my "friends". When I could not find flesh and blood humans to share my interests, I searched out their books with the same fervor that a starving man searches for food! Authors are always willing to talk about the subjects that are near and dear to their hearts, and are always looking for us "seekers" of their precious information. Its a marriage made in heaven!

A friend who knew about my own passionate seeking after the secrets of sound, music, and color, had told me that I needed to know a friend of his whose works I would find most fascinating. When he said that we were birds of the same feather I knew I had to find her books.

Dr. Valerie Hunt is one of those Authors who has faithfully shared her vast treasure of knowledge about the Science of Sound, and Color, and the Human Vibrations of Consciousness.

Wow! A new "Friend"! Excitement leaped up the moment I saw the writing on her book, "Infinite Mind: Science of the Human Vibrations of Consciousness". I knew I had a "treasure" in my hands!

I settled into my lawn chair for a wonderful morning with my new like-minded "Friend". It didn't take long, ..., there it was, on page three, ..., that first "A-Ha" moment.

"In the early 1970's, I was teaching a graduate seminar on the neuromuscular aspects of behavior. In addition to discussing research *discoveries, I questioned the vast array of common human experiences that seemed to defy rational understanding, or to lie beyond the scope of scientific inquiry. I suggested that these experiences must have some deep, hidden reality because they contained such sensory, motor, cognitive and emotional stimuli. Certainly the label "imagined" didn't fit. Though my comments were casual, at times it was as if I had lit the fuses of stored fireworks. The class enlivened...."*

Dr. Valerie Hunt, Infinite Mind: Science of the Human Vibrations of Consciousness", pages 2-3

That phrase, **"stored fireworks"** lit something down deep in my bones!

Yes! That's **IT!**

Something happened
    When I read it,
        Truth was hidden,
            But this fed it;

>There's a message here,
>>And I can't shed it,
>>>And I really
>>>>Have to spread it, ...,

Oh, I **do** feel a poem coming on, ...,

www.pacepublishing.com

FIREWORKS!!!

There are "***Fireworks***" stored
    In the "inners" of man
        And they're surfacing now
            Just as fast
                As they can.

They're exploding
    With fervor
        That can't be denied; ...;
            Bubbling up
                From the places
                    We've sent them
                      To hide.

All the feelings
    We tried
        To ignore, ...,
            And forget, ...,
        Are demanding
             Attention, ...,
                ..., We're afraid to, ...,
                  ..., And yet, ...,

We will find,
    If we let them rise up
        And escape,
            The effect
                On our health
                    Will make us
                        Stand up
                          And gape!!

We'll see "Miracles" happen,
    And find Our peace
        Restored,
            So the Blessings
                Of Life
                    Just cannot
                        Be ignored!

All those blockages stopped
    Our great "**Fireworks**" display
        For we couldn't
            Get Our "Fire"
                To Our "works"
                    In a way
    That would light up
        The darkness
            That we have created
    In a world
        Where that darkness
            Has been over rated.

But now that
    We're learning
        To let that all go,
    And we're choosing
        A Pathway
            We've wanted to know,
        That leads to The Truth
            Of humanity's roots
                And that fills us with Joy
                While we all
                    Are en route,

We'll embrace
> The "new" knowledge
>> That we've long forgotten
>>> And abandon
>>>> The ways
>>>>> We've been taught
>>>>>> That were rotten;

And we'll gird up
> Our loins
>> With the power
>>> Of Truth,
>>> And we'll
>>>> **Broadcast**
>>>>> That Truth
>>>>>> From Man's
>>>>>>> Projection Booth!

And We'll MAKE "**Something**"
> From "**Nothing**", ...,
>> At least, "Nothing" that's **seen**;
>>> For We'll generate
>>>> *P O W E R*
>>>>> From Our
>>>>>> On-board machine

That connects
> To The **Source**
>> Of **ALL** Power
>>> And Might.
>>>> Now **THAT**
>>>>> Kind of "**Fireworks**"
>>>>>> Is just WAY
>>>>>>> Out'ta sight!!

Nothing in Our Earthbound Mind
    Can conceive
        Of the pyrotechnics
            Spirit Children believe
    Can be unleashed
        From deep
            Within Our True Being
        That will bring forth
            Creations
                We'll all soon
                    Be seeing.

We're awakening,
    And,
        We're remembering
            Our Stuff!!
                And We're finding
                    Our Strengths
                        To be MORE
                            Than enough

To repair
    And replace
        All the "stuff"
            That's been broken,
                While We struggled
                    Through Life
                        Thinking We're
                            A mere token

Of a species
>That somehow
>>Can walk on two legs,
>>>And must now
>>>>Bumble through
>>>>>What is left
>>>>>>Of life's dregs.

We've forgotten
>The "*Fireworks*"
>>That are stored
>>>Within <u>**Us**</u>,
>>>>And We're tired
>>>>>Of aaaalllllllll
>>>>>>Of the **muss**
>>>>>>>And the ***fuss***

Of a life
>That is broken
>>And hard to endure,
>>>When We know
>>>>That Our "*Fireworks*"
>>>>>Can create
>>>>>>**Something More**

Than this **Humdrum**
    Existence,
        That is fragile, at best,
            When We know
                Deep within Us
    That We're **MORE**
        Than the rest
            Of the victimized weaklings
                That fawn, …,
                    …, And they grovel,
            Thinking **this** *is Life's best, …,*
                Oh, **P L E A S E !!**
                    Give me a shovel!!

We *forgot*
    That We're **'gods"**
        Having **made** *Ourselves "lesser",*
            So We'd **fit**
                Here on Earth!! …!
                    …! For a **"god"**
                        That's a **stresser**!!!

Where We once
    Were magnificent
        Beings of Light,
            We have **MADE** OURSELVES
                Less; …;
                    …; We *forgot*
                        All Our **Might!!**

But Our Mem'ry
   Is o-pen-ing up
      To the **ruse**
         That Our Life **cannot** be
            Anything
               That We choose!!!

We're remembering
   "***Fireworks***"
      That We **saw**,
         And We ***did***,
            Long before
               There was Earth,
                  And the Moon
                     Was a kid,

And remembering **WHO**
   We once were,
      Long ago,
         Before density struck,
            And Our Light
               Became low,

And **Our con-nec-tion**
   To ***All-That-Is***
      Was **obscured**
         By the struggles and hurts,
            And the wounds
               We've endured!!!

So, Listen up!!
    Open Your Heart
        And Your Mind, ...,

            And **become**
                One
                    Of The **Creative** Kind

        That **releases**
           Those "**Fireworks**"
              Stored deep
                  In Your Soul,

        And then,
            Make Your Life **Show**
              That You're
                  Every whit whole

By the way that You **live**,
    And the things
        That You **do**
           So that others will see it,
              And they'll grab a clue
        And begin to remember
           THEIR "**Fireworks**"
           Within,
    And before long,
        We'll **ALL**
           Be **beginning**
                Again!!!!

                Vanessa Conaway Pace
            May 25, 2013, Lynnwood, Washington

Fireworks!!!

**This Is Your
Invitation
To Create!**

Dear Seeker of Those "Deeper Things",

So, There You **ARE**, ...,
    "Fireworks",
        All set to explode. ....
            But, somehow
                The fuse
                    Got left
                        Way down the road.

But **The Creative Winds**
    Have Their **Own**
        Set of matches,
            And they'll blow
                Upon **You**
                    Until Your "*fire*"
                      Catches!

So, You just may as well
    Let it
        Warm up
            Your heart, ...
                ..., And then,
                    Pick up Your tools
                        And get ready
                          To start!

Now Its YOUR Turn To Be "Creator"!
Put YOUR Thoughts Here, and Read Them Later!

Yes, You ARE
       The Creator
              With the "***Fireworks***" within.
                    Now begin
                            Your Great Project, ...,
                                You'll be sure
                                      That You will win!

Now Its YOUR Turn To Be "Creator"!
Put YOUR Thoughts Here, and Read Them Later!

Now Its YOUR Turn To Be "Creator"!
Put YOUR Thoughts Here, and Read Them Later!

Now Its YOUR Turn To Be "Creator"!
Put YOUR Thoughts Here, and Read Them Later!

FOCUS

www.pacepublishing.com

FOCUS
Inspirational Background

*H*e was a BIG ex-Marine, ..., the kind you say "Yes, SIR!" to as you sprint with all haste to follow his barked commands. After many years of service in that capacity he was now back with his family and community, and using many of the skills he had learned as a Drill Instructor to sharpen up the ranks of his new audiences.

I arrived early to one of his Lectures to get a good seat, to listen, and to learn. As an experienced Lecturer myself, I settled in to observe the back-of-the-room preliminaries as the rest of the audience trickled in.

My ears perked up when I noticed our Lecturer talking secretively to a bunch of teen-aged boys. I've raised a couple of teenagers, and I recognized the conspiratorial smirks on their faces. They were obviously going to get to do something ornery, and they had adult permission. .... no, ..., **instruction**, to do it. They were enjoying the intrigue.

I didn't know what the "plot" was, but all of my antennae were up. Something was obviously going to happen, and I wanted to be ahead of the "game".

The appointed time arrived, and the Lecture began with a carefully laid down outline of the evening's plan. In typical Marine Drill Instructor fashion he followed the famous formula: "Tell 'em what you're gonna tell 'em. Tell 'em. Tell 'em what you told 'em." He told us what he was going to tell us, and forewarned us that there would be things brought out in his presentation that we **needed** to know. They would be valuable to us.

Then, in typical active-duty story fashion, he told us how the Marines win battles: ...: They **"FOCUS"** on the desired outcome. The Marine in battle must not allow the mind to wonder, "What's for dinner?". That one little luxury of a thought that was not in line with the goal could mean that quite possibly **"they"** would become someone else's dinner, and the desired objective would be lost. **"FOCUS"** was definitely the key to their success.

Our ex-DI had obviously trained many new recruits to "**FOCUS**" on the goal at hand, and we were just new members of his latest "Boot Camp". He intended to be successful. He was on familiar ground.

A new recruit must be aware of the dangers of not paying attention when important information is being given out. He warned us about how easy it is to let the mind wander and get bogged down in the details, or to be distracted by other things that seem to demand our attention. And he carefully admonished us that if we did not stay alert to the purpose we had gathered there for we could miss the most important things that we came there to learn. Pearls of wisdom don't always fly around a second time.

Then the Lecture began in earnest. I took notes, and made myself track with his teachings, but all the while, in the back of my mind, my senses were on high alert. Something was going to happen. Those teenagers had been primed for a purpose. I would pass the test!

He carefully laid the groundwork of his teaching, and, just at the time when the details would have put me to sleep, I saw him give the signal. Bunches of teenagers jumped to their feet, climbed over chairs, upended anything that would move, and yelled at the tops of their voices. It was at that moment that the Lecturer gave the punchline. That was when he gave the core of his teaching, and revealed the nugget of the valuable thing that we had come there to learn. But those who were easily distracted by outside circumstances, or by what some would call "The Shiny Thing Syndrome", missed the meat in the meal.

When the distraction started, having been forewarned that some mischief was afoot, I "**FOCUS**"ed in on the man and the message, and I got the goodies!!! Truth be known, after the mayhem settled down, I was one of two, out of the whole audience, that could raise my hand to answer the question that only those who were listening could have answered. The fine art of "**FOCUS**" had saved the day for me.

That powerful example was a more sophisticated version of what my Father taught me as a little girl in the red raspberry patch on our farm. The days were hot, and the long rows of plants bending low under the weight of so many ripened berries were a discouraging sight to my young eyes. How could I ever pick all of those berries? Daddy's unsympathetic answer to my wailings was, "Just keep your hands going toward the bucket". That's the West Virginia version of **"FOCUS"** on the task at hand, and soon it will be done.

Many times in my life, as I have sought to get through the humdrum chores of the day, or to complete some impossible work assignment, or to persevere under adverse circumstances in order to accomplish one of my dreams, my Father's wonderful voice speaks from that sunny day on the hillside, ..., "Just keep your hands going toward the bucket".

Then, later in my life, when greater Truths started to open up to me, I found the same basic principle at work in the field of Success in Business teachings, in the examples of the lives of the Great Masters of Music and the Arts and Sciences, and in the field of Quantum Physics, which began to show me how things in our neck of the

Universe really work. Since I was the little girl always following my Father around on the farm asking, "How does that work, Daddy?", this newfound treasure trove of knowledge helped to scratch that constant itch to know and understand this world that I had come to, and how to make it tick. They all pointed in the same direction:

- We create our own life and our own reality;
- The only thing we have complete and total control (*"FOCUS"*) over is our own mind;
- Whatever we *"FOCUS"* on manifests as a reality in our life, whether we want it or not;
- Our mind considers our thoughts as its command, and immediately responds, "Okay! Can do! ...!", and then it finds a way to do it; and, if we're smart, we'll
- *"FOCUS"* beyond the problem, and begin to think consciously on where we want to go.

Wonder of wonders, here we were, back at the same message that our lecturing ex-Marine DI had given: *"FOCUS"* I had heard it said long ago that if we would all *"FOCUS"* on one thing that we desired, as one united thought-group we could create it almost immediately! Somehow inside I knew that was true, but how to do it?

Things don't just happen by magic, ..., or, ..., DO they?! **Hmmmmmm**. If we all did agree on something that we really wanted, and it actually happened (as many scientifically documented experiments have proven to do... (See "The Intention Experiment".), then, what was the **mechanism** that actually made it happen?

  Enter Lynne McTaggart, and others, with their explanations of the Quantum Field, and the electromagnetic waves and frequencies set up by our thoughts and intentions. But those luscious shiny pieces in our collective **"Kaleidoscope"** must wait for another time, because The Muses beckon, and, ...,

  ..., I feel a poem coming on!!!

www.pacepublishing.com

FOCUS

Just "*FOCUS*"
    Your thoughts
        And Your feelings
            On the way **You**
                Would have it to be

In **Your** world,
    And Yourself,
        Dust those Plans
            Off the shelf,
                And then
                    CONCENTRATE
                      On what You **SEE**.

Hold that prayer!
    Stand Your ground!
        Others have
            And have found
                That Their efforts
                    Don't go unrewarded,

And that "God"
    Does respond
        To that bond
            They have spawned,
            And that
                EVERYTHING
                Can be
                    "Afforded".

There's no charge
>For the things
>>That Your Mind
>>>Starts to bring
>>>>From the plasma
>>>>>That's out there
>>>>>>In space.

Its just waiting
>For **YOU**
>>To direct
>>>All that "goo"
>>>>Into something
>>>>>That **YOU**
>>>>>>Put in place!

Yes, The **"System's"** designed
>With **YOUR pleasure**
>>In mind
>>>So that **WE**
>>>>Could have all
>>>>>That **WE** needed;

But **WE** listened
>To those
>>Who lead **US**
>>>By the nose;
>>>>Now **WE** think
>>>>>That **OUR** case
>>>>>>Must be
>>>>>>>**"Pleaded"**.

That's **SOOOOOO** far
    From **The Truth!**
        It was all
            A big spoof
                To make **US**
                    Think our Minds
                        Were extraneous.

So, remember
    Your craft, ...
        ..., All those others
            Are daft! ...!
                And their Crimes
                    And distortions
                        Are heinous!!!!

Its Your thoughts
    And intentions
        That make **things**
            Change dimensions,
                And Your **"FOCUS"**
                    On them
                      Makes it happen,

So, weed out
    All those thoughts
        That are costing
            You LOTS,
                And then **"FOCUS"**
                    And Don't be caught
                        Nappin'!!!

Use the eyes
    Deep inside
        To envision your ride
            (And You'll know
                This is **NOT** hokus pokus)!

Its the Wisdom
    Of the Ages
        That was used
            By The Sages, ...
        Sooooo,

                "FOCUS",

                    "FOCUS",

                        "FOCUS"!!!

                      Vanessa Conaway Pace
            January 13, 2007, Seattle, Washington

FOCUS

> *This Is Your Invitation To Create!*

Dear Seeker of Those "Deeper Things",

You had an **idea**
    That excited You **lots,**
        But then, other thoughts
        Lead you to
            Other plots;

And **that**
        Spread out your **"FOCUS"**
        Into weak
            Scattershot's.

But now **that** idea
    Has arisen again,
        But this time You have
      A new **yen**
        To begin,

And a fervor that says
    I **MUST** do it **NOW,**
        For its my unique passion....
      ..., Now **that's**
      A real
          WOW!!!

Now Its YOUR Turn To Be "Creator"!
Put YOUR Thoughts Here, and Read Them Later!

Passion! Passion!
    That's the fashion
        That will bring
            The new design for YOU!

Passion!
    Keep your strong
        Com-passion
            For the thing
                That made Your Heart
                    Feel that work anew!

Now Its YOUR Turn To Be "Creator"!
Put YOUR Thoughts Here, and Read Them Later!

Now Its YOUR Turn To Be "Creator"!
Put YOUR Thoughts Here, and Read Them Later!

Now Its YOUR Turn To Be "Creator"!
Put YOUR Thoughts Here, and Read Them Later!

The Crys-tal-line Sea

www.pacepublishing.com

The Crys-tal-line Sea
Inspirational Background

I tend to seek after the writings, and broadcasts, and artistic creations of gifted people who have had the courage and stick-to-it-iveness to pursue the study and development of their particular gifting. Those who have been sensitive enough to follow the leadings of that little Voice within them, and have chosen to lay down the more frivolous pursuits of life in favor of polishing up the diamond within them, will surely find the pot o' gold at the end of their rainbow! They have responded to the tugs of hungry souls crying "teach me", and have elected to share their insights with the Awakening world, and they are treasures. Yes! I am looking for YOU, so that I can grow with a well-rounded understanding and appreciation of both the world to which I have come, and of the one that I chose to lay down in order to qualify for this Earthly trip!

Many names of these faithful ones, and their precious teachings come to mind.

American author Dr. Carolyn Myss is one who has paid such a price in order to add her light beam to the ever-expanding Stream that is illuminating our current darkness. She caught my attention with one little story she shared in one of her books. It seems that she, basking in the untried arrogance of institutional study, found herself quite bored with the quiet delivery of the peaceful old "Sage" who was delivering a lecture on changing the world. Dr. Myss approached the venerable "Sage" after his lecture, and, with great patience, in response to her pressuring insistence of how she was going to change the world from her ivory tower of education, he gently admonished her that the best thing she could do for the world was to heal **herself**! That may seem rather unglamorous to those of us with grandiose visions about our own powerful (and highly visible) influence upon the world that we live in.

Both Dr. Myss and the "Sage" had found themselves in the right place at the right time to steer her life in a direction that has enriched her own life, the personal lives of many, and the collective life of our Awakening Family.

The Wisdom of that "Sage's" message had a ring of Truth in it, but how to **implement** it, ..., without losing our zeal to accomplish those things we contracted to do when we arrived here, or being relegated to the dustbin of ignominy!

Then, while researching the state-of-the-art technology in dentistry, I came upon the teachings of Russian scientists Arkady Petrov, Grigori Grabovoi, Svetlana Smirnova, and others who were publishing testimonies of the actual **regrowth** of teeth that had been removed, and of the regeneration of organs of the body that were either diseased or had been surgically removed!!! Now **that** caught my attention! I had been expecting news of breakthroughs of this creative nature because I had been told long ago that this was coming.

The year was 1983 and I had just left my diabetic husband resting in the hospital on the eve of the scheduled amputation of his right leg at the hip. **Devastation** was demanding that I would allow it to sink its miserable claws into every fiber of my being; but, that indomitable Seed of self-determination that is planted in all of us was struggling to sprout within Me.

There was nothing more that I could do at the hospital. I was told that our fate was irrevocably sealed, and that I must just accept that horrific mindset as fact, and learn to live with it. But that incorruptible "Seed" within me somehow just would not let me crumble. So, I took our two children, and a mountain of laundry that had accumulated during the desperate days of his illness, and went to an all-night laundromat near the hospital.

My good and faithful friend had handed me a tape that day of a prophetic word that had been given before a large Convention by a man of recognized spiritual sensitivity. In my experience I had known his track record to be good. His teachings on the power of the spoken word had echoed my Mother's insistence that I be wise with my words because they have a creative power. No teenage slang for me! I must find the correct words to express my feelings, demands, and ideas!

So, I tucked a cassette player into the laundry basket, summoned all the self-control I could muster, and went about this mundane task of life, while disciplining myself to believe that something good was going to happen.

With the laundry in, and the children safely sleeping in the station wagon that was clearly in view through the open door of the strip mall laundromat, I slipped the tape into the machine, hoping for some respite from the almost debilitating pain of that unfolding life experience.

His words broke through my pain like mighty shots of adrenaline! There was a promise from something I instinctively knew I could believe in, ..., an awakening to a primal Truth, and a clarion call to action in the proclamation that declared that, "We are coming into the time when limbs and organs that have been surgically removed **will be restored**!" And then, the clincher, which admonished that, "You are a little behind in this", followed by the reminder that it could have happened long ago, had We been doing our part to implement the "System" that is already in place; ...; **We** just have to throw the switch! And, the power to throw that switch resides <u>**ONLY IN US!!!**</u>

Ahh! A faint glimmer of hope! "Words" of promise that threw some much sought for fertilizer on that "indomitable Seed" within Me that was scanning the universe for anything that would lessen my desperation.

By a lot of Grace and determination I survived the storm, and we came out of the crisis with what would be called a "miracle" by all reasonable standards. But, the force of my "indomitable Seed" kept scanning the universe for the **WAY** that promise of restoration would be implemented. What was the methodology? I needed something that would awaken within me the memory of how the "System" really works.

Another author "friend" came to the rescue. I got another piece of the picture from Dr. Robert Becker's "Body Electric" book. Dr. Becker writes that he thought about the fact that when the lowly salamander loses a tail, or a limb, it simply **regrows** a new one. Well then, why shouldn't a high creation like **Man** be able to do the same thing?

Dr. Becker's brilliant research found the secret of the salamander: ...: The salamander uses electrical impulses to stimulate the regrowth. Then this inspired researcher reasoned that the body of Man is "electric", so why wouldn't that same salamander principle work in Man? Since all truth is parallel, I was knowing more and more that there are some vital principles here that we need to understand, ..., if We are going to responsibly step into our assigned role of "co-creators".

I was making progress in my quest for the answers to how things really work! And then, in seeking answers for the healing and restoration of teeth, I stumbled on the website, books, and teaching videos of the remarkable regeneration of human organs and teeth discovered, produced, and taught around the world by Russian scientist/philosopher Dr. Arkady Petrov. He had discovered the knowledge of principles for creation and healing contained in the ancient and modern literature!

Wow! Help was on the way! Hope was brightening. ... But, Oh, drat! All three of his books were only available in his native Russian language! More delays. I put a little of my own pressure on the universe to supply my need, and, as the old adage says, "All good things come to those who wait.", ..., five years later I discovered that they were now available in English! Who says that we can't have what we want?!

And, I found more explanations in the works of another Russian academician, Dr. Grigori Grabovoi,, Doctor of mathematics, physics, applied mechanics and medicine, and Head of the "International Program for health improvement of man", who has published many books explaining the restorative principles, and the methodology behind the "Sage" of Dr. Carolyn Myss' experience, who said that the best thing that she could do for the universe was to heal herself. Grabovoi comes at the healing of personal issues from the perspective that Einstein espoused in his famous quote that warns that "you cannot solve a problem from the same level that created it". **We have to come at the problem from a higher perspective.** Grabovoi quotes the Ancient Law that states that, "Anyone who acts on behalf of **everyone** receives from the Creator his do".

There it is! Finally a "methodology". When we set our intentions upon the healing, or deliverance, or blessing of **all**, then our own personal need for that will be met! We are simply a microcosm of the macrocosm of the universe (See the following poem.) When we fix the big picture then the fragments within it will fall into the Parental order! When we put each of the torn threads of the Tapestry back in place, and that **must** be done one thread at a time, then the whole picture is healed.

I get it! We thought that We all had to physically come together (like soccer crowds), and somehow get everybody to think alike (like political parties), and, of course, we would need to have those who were more powerful than us present so we'd know exactly what to do, ..., and then just **maybe** we could fix some of this Earth and its inhabitants' problems.

But, NO!!! Each person can quietly, peacefully, and confidently tie his own loose strings, and the Tapestry of our individual and collective Life will be beautiful once again!

That's definitely going to make life exciting..... I **do** feel a poem coming on!

www.pacepublishing.com

The Crys-tal-line Sea

You're a mi-cro-cosm
    Of the U-ni-verse!
        It couldn't get better
            And it couldn't get worse.

E-very-**thing** that **You**
    De-cided to **BE**
        Could be pulled
           From what's stored
                In **"The Crys-tal-line Sea"**!

While You started out Pure
    In the essence of **Love**,
        You have had to endure
           Living **OUT**
                Of that Glove.

As You've walked
    Out Your Path
        In dimensions of Time
           You have taken a bath
                In this lower field's grime!

When The "Light",
    (Which is where
        We all **wanted** to be,)
           Turned to "dark"
               (With some help
                    From **"Ill-lumin-a-ti."**)

We were **stuck**
    In this lo-wer
        Di-men-sion-al mist
            Where its **tough**
                For a **Being of Love**
                    To exist!

We allowed "Them"
    To keep Us
        In slav-er-y's fist,
            When We could
                Have responded
                    Like The One Judas kissed!

For We had all the tools
    That We needed to win,
        But We **thought**
            On the "dark"
                And it sucked us
                    Right in.

We were **"Light"**
    'Til they snipped
        All our DNA back, ...,
            E-ven **THAT**
                We **ALLOWED**
                    So We'd fit
                        In Earth's sack.

For We'd plotted
    Our course,
        And We'd set
            Our Intention
                To experience Life
                    In this Earthbound
                        Dimension.

Now, We've DONE THAT,
    And We
        Got the T-shirt
            For Sure!

And We're ready
    To cry out,
        "Okay!
            Nothing more!"

We've decided that **We**
    Liked it best
        Where We've come from,
        And that **We**
            Want Life **here**
                To be like **Home**,
                    And then some!

And We **know**
    We can have it
        As long as We'll
            THINK,
                Not on what
                    "THEY have tried; ...;

              THAT brought Earth
                  To the brink!

But We'll **THINK**
> On the "things"
>> That We've **WANTED**
>>> To be,

And We'll ***draw out***
> Those "things"
>> From **"The Crys-tal-line Sea"**.

For, **Our THOUGHTS**
> Have created
>> This mess
>>> That We're in. ....
>>>> Being "**gods**"
>>>>> We can ***change that!***

Let The Future **BEGIN!!!!!!!**

You're a mi-cro-cosm

    Of the U-ni-verse!

        It couldn't get better

            And it couldn't get worse.

    E-very-**thing** that **You**

        De-cided to **BE**

            Could be pulled

                From what's stored

                    In "The Crys-tal-line Sea"!

                        Vanessa Conaway Pace
              January 13, 2007, Seattle, Washington

www.pacepublishing.com

The Crys-tal-line Sea

> **This Is Your Invitation To Create!**

Dear Seeker of Those "Deeper Things",

Many **treasures**
    Are **stored**
        In the oceans
            Of Earth;
              But ***imagine***
                  What those
                      In **The BIG Sea**
                          Are worth!

Never mind
    Mining **here**,
        In these lower
            Dimensions; ...,
                Where You'll doubt
                    What You'll find,
                        And have great
                            Apprehensions;

But, ...,
    Cast your net **There**,
        In "**The Crystalline Sea**",
        And **become**,
            Everything
                That You've wanted
                To **Be**!

Now Its YOUR Turn To Be "Creator"!
Put YOUR Thoughts Here, and Read Them Later!

Yes, the power is within you
  To create something new,
    So, get out Your Book,
      And Your Pen
        And Just DO!

Now Its YOUR Turn To Be "Creator"!
Put YOUR Thoughts Here, and Read Them Later!

Now Its YOUR Turn To Be "Creator"!
Put YOUR Thoughts Here, and Read Them Later!

Now Its YOUR Turn To Be "Creator"!
Put YOUR Thoughts Here, and Read Them Later!

Ill-lumen-a-ti

www.pacepublishing.com

Ill-lumen-a-ti
Inspirational Background

We are told by Poets and Songwriters, and, even some Scientists, that "Love" makes the world go round, and that may be true. But, if it is true, then my question is, why does the concept of "Love" only seem to **apply** these days in the fields of poetry, theology, and romance? We pretty much know, and accept, the meaning of "Love" in poetry and theology, but things get a little muddy in our thinking when we try to figure out exactly what it means in today's concept of "romance". In that context it seems to mean different things to different people. I checked out the definition of "romance" in the current on-line dictionary, and it read, "A strong, sometimes short-lived attachment, fascination, or enthusiasm for something: ...". I found that interesting because my 1928 edition of Funk & Wagnalls Practical Standard Dictionary defines "romance" as, "To indulge in visionary fabrications; tell fanciful stories.". None of those definitions ever mentioned the word "Love".

If "**Love**" really is such a powerful force, then wouldn't you think that, in addition to the poetic, theologic, and romantic areas of our lives, "Love" should also be making all the other areas of our life go round? It seems to me that, if that were truly the case, we'd all be living in Hog Heaven, and We would be contentedly declaring that life is beautiful.

When I scan the present reality that much of the world is looking at it doesn't seem to really show that. As a matter of fact, the "news" coming out of most media seems more to resemble the "visionary fabrications" and "tell fanciful stories" of the 1928 dictionary definition of "romance"!

So, that immediately made me think about the discomforts and fears that many people are currently experiencing. And again I ask the question, "If the old poetic adage is correct, and "Love" really does make the world go round, then why aren't things running more smoothly? And, why aren't the world's peoples deliriously happy? Even a cursory look shows that the wheels seem to be coming off the wagons that are pulling our society with downhill speed. For instance, why don't we feel safe and securely protected within the embrace of governments, politics, and, obviously, finance, banking, and the economy? Why don't We routinely hear about how much our banker "Loves" us?! Or, how much our government "Loves" us?! If "Love" is supposed to be the "force" that makes the world go round, why aren't we actually experiencing it! I want to live in a world where We can TRUST the ENERGIES that are making it go round!

And, if "Love" is the force that makes the world go round, as the old poetic adage says, and if we are not seeing it in our governmental, or political, or financial, or banking, or economic arenas, then it is fair to ask, "What **IS** the force that is making those fields go round?" They **CAN"T** run without some kind of a "force" behind them! Nothing happens without some kind of **ENERGY** making it happen. (See poem, **"Its The ENERGY You Send Out"**, in this Volume.) Some of us can't even get OURSELVES going without our coffee, or our **ENERGY** drinks to power us on to the next **ENERGY** boost! So, why would those world-wide conglomerates be any different?

Just as I suspected, ..., since we do not seem to be experiencing the warm fuzzy feelings of "Love" coming to us through our daily contact with the systems that so strongly impact our lives today, then logically **there has to be another force that is behind the events of the collective milieu that we live in.** What is THAT force? ...? And, how did it get so in control of our lives? Surely We would not have deliberately created a society that is missing that all-important "Love" ingredient, ..., Or, **did** we?

Could it be that, in our pursuit of the things that we **THOUGHT** were important, or, even in our desperate attempt to keep ourselves and our families afloat in these difficult days, we simply **forgot** who we really **ARE** on the inside? Or, maybe its just that We did not have the time or ENERGY to find out if and how we can change things that we don't want? We've been a little distracted by all the pressures that seem to be whirling around us. Could it be that We simply did not have enough ENERGY left at the end of our day to even think about, never mind **USE,** the "AWESOMENESS" within our own innate Celestial Being to manage ourselves and our environment into the "Peace on Earth" that we have been waiting for? Or, maybe We were taught that we had to wait for **someone else** to create it **for** us?

If that's really the case, then we can't really **blame** others for taking over and running things for "Their" own profit. Word has it that WE are the ones that WE have been waiting for to fix the mess that has been created while We were busy with other things!

Rats! Its back to "**Me**", and "**Us**" again! The Masters and Teachers that have been sent to us throughout the ages have taught that the power and authority to create what we want lies within us. Therefore, we can't even get angry at, or even be judgmental of, the ones who stepped into the "Love" void that We have been allowing, and created some very unacceptable conditions for us to live under. **Double "Rats!".** We needed SOMEONE to blame!

And then, **here's the real clincher**: Those same Masters and Teachers that taught us about the depth of "Love" that is available to Us clearly admonished Us that, everything that does not resonate with the "Love" frequency will **have** to disintegrate because of the laws governing ENERGY. And, when that inevitably happens, "They" further admonish us that **WE** who have been living under "Their" loveless tyrannies MUST NOT rejoice at "Their" calamities, because "Love" wouldn't do that! **THAT**'s the true test that WE surely want to pass. The question that faces us is, "Will We be able to "Love" our fellow Hu-mans enough to recognize their fallibilities, unconditionally forgive them, release them to their earned rewards, and quickly get on with the rebuilding of our beautiful world with the "Love" ENERGY that We have thereby released?" That "force" will create a world that is truly powered by "Love"!!!

Hmmmm! And all the while We thought that We were going to get to find those culprits that have been making our lives miserable, and "nail 'em to the wall", and then life would be beautiful; when all the while the truth was lurking: We all came from the same Source. And, the **Truth** is that **"We" are ALL greatly "Loved", and, therefore, will be given endless opportunities to make different choices in "Our" lives, until "We" ALL are ONE within that "Love" frequency!**

Ohhhh! I really DO feel a poem coming on!!!

Ill-lumin-a-ti

There's a group
    That's called
        "Ill-lumin-a-ti"
            That has gotten
                A little bit **Haugh-ty,**
                    (And their antics
                        Are just downright
                            Naugh-ty!)

They have **plundered**
    And **burned,**
        Lived on monies
            WE'VE earned,
                And **WE'RE** feeling
                      Its **time**
                          They were
                              Caugh'ty!!!

They've had
    The **power**
        Of the **purse,**
            And **things**
                Couldn't be worse
                    In the world
                        That "**cabal**" has
                            Controlled.

They **made wars,**
    Stole Our gold,
        Wielded powers
            Untold,
                And they'd best
                    Mend their ways
                        Or they'll **rot-ty!**

If You're lookin'
    For **who**
        Got Us into this stew,
            And **You're** willing
                To say that
                    WE <u>LET</u> 'EM,

Then **You** <u>also</u> can say
        "Its the **END**
            Of their day,"
                And can **give**
                    The command
                To **GO**

                        GET 'EM!!!

There'll be help
    From above
        (Yes, its tempered
            By Love!)
                That has watched
                    As these "**Ill**" winds
                        Blew no good,

"Help's" been *waiting*
    For **US**
        To **unite**
            In this **fuss**
                And to **take**
                    All the actions
                        That **WE** *could.*

Now **We've** *made*
    Our *wants known*
        In a **unified groan**, ...,
            ..., *And all Heaven*
                Has joined in
                    That sigh,
And have given
    Relief
        And **rejoiced** *that*
            That thief
                Will **NO LONGER**
                    Make people cry!

All the monies
    They took,
        All the nations
             They shook,
                All the lies
                    That they told
                        To the people,

Will be **rectified now,**
    'Cause **We're NOT GONNA BOW,**
        And, **We're No longer under**
            Their steeple!!!

Yes, they lied
    In **that**, too,
        Said **We** came
            Out of "goo"
                And denied
                    That **We're "gods"**
                        Here from Heaven.

Said **We**
    Had to be "saved"
        Because **We**
             Were depraved,
                And were "sinners"
                    And all of that **"leaven"**.

Its a means of
    Control
        When they mess
            With your soul.
                Now **that** plan
                    Is consistently battered.

They will learn,
    In their turn,
        What you sow
            You **WILL** earn,
                And the things
                    That they **did**
                        Really mattered!

All the **fortunes**
    They gathered,
        All the **"storms"**
            That they weathered
                Were not worth
                    All the plots
                        And the scheming,

For **The Truth**
    Has been told
        (Now **THAT's**
            The **Real Gold**!)

    And the world knows
        They're **NOT**
            What they're seeming!

This has been
    A long trip,
        And they're **choosing**
            To **ship**
                All their mess
                    Off to some other planet,

Where **WE**
    Won't be involved.
        Good!
            That problem's
                Been **solved**
                    For **Our unified thought**
                        Has said, **"Can it!"**

This is **Our** world
    To steer,
        WE don't want
            Your stuff here,
                WE want ***Love***,
                    Peace, and ***Joy***
                        In Our midst.

And, if **You**
    Can't do **that**
        We'll take **You**
            To the mat!
                Its a ***scourge***
                    WE'VE decided
                        We're "ridst"!

We've had
    Power to **THINK**
        What **WE** want
            In this stink
                They've created
                    By greed
                        And corruption,

But We've **thought**
    On the ***rot***
        That this lot
            Has brought
                And, **OUR THOUGHT**
                    Put that lot
                        In production.

Now We *think*
    On **WHAT's <u>SOUGHT</u>**
        And the answer
           That's brought
              Is that **God's**
                  Got that lot
                      In reduction!!!

They've been snared
    By their words
        SooOOOO,
            Those arrogant birds
                Caught
                      Themselves
                        In a Cosmic
                          Eruption!!!!

(Bye, Guys!
Thanks for playing Your part
As the dark side of Us
So well
That it made Us
DECIDE
We want **Love** and **LIGHT**,
And to stop all the pain!!!!!
Good Job!!!!
See 'ya in the distant future,
when **You** have decided
that **You** want **Love** and **LIGHT**, too.
Then, We'll all be together again!!!!!!)

Vanessa Conaway Pace
January 13-14, 2007, Seattle, Washington

Ill-lumen-a-ti

This Is Your Invitation To Create!

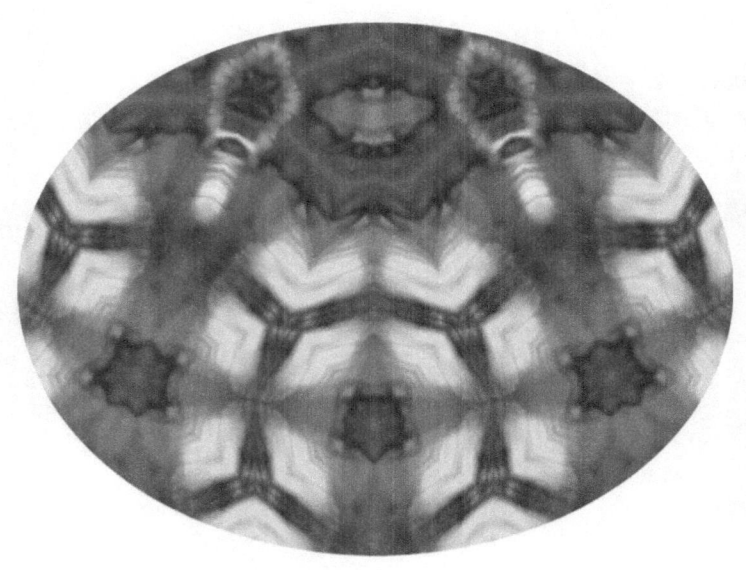

Dear Seeker of Those "Deeper Things",

Okay!!! ...!!!
    So We found
        That **some** bumps
            In Our roads
                Were caused
                    By some **ghouls**
                        From **a different**
                            Source code.

But, **We're**
    From a **different**
        Area code,
            And We carry inside Us
                A different pay load
                    That's **unfolded** as We
                        Travel over
                            Life's road.

Sooooo, make sure
    That **You're** using
        The **mode**
            Of your load
                To help Earth's **whole** shipload
                    Enjoy
                        "**The High Road**"!
                        (See Poem
                        Page 283.)

Now Its YOUR Turn To Be "Creator"!
Put YOUR Thoughts Here, and Read Them Later!

We could have been building
    This world all along,
        If we had been using
            The Words of our Song
                To create all the things
                    That we've wanted to see,
                        And then we could all
                          Have lived happily!

Now Its YOUR Turn To Be "Creator"!
Put YOUR Thoughts Here, and Read Them Later!

Now Its YOUR Turn To Be "Creator"!
Put YOUR Thoughts Here, and Read Them Later!

Now Its YOUR Turn To Be "Creator"!
Put YOUR Thoughts Here, and Read Them Later!

In A Parallel Universe
In A Parallel Universe

www.pacepublishing.com

In A Parallel Universe
Inspirational Background

*I*s it **"de-ja-vu"**,
    Or a **"flip"**
        That You do
            Between **this**
                And some **other**
                    Universes

That are said
    To exist, ...,
        ..., That's a **"fact"**
            That We've missed
                In the teachings
                    Our "Science"
                        Rehearses!

But there's
    Too many cases
        Of people's being
            In places,
                And surroundings
                    Of different
                        Dimensions

And claim **you**
    To be "there",
        When We all
            Are aware
                That You're **HERE**, ...,
                    ..., Causing great
                        Apprehensions!

Is it just because
>   **Your thinking**
>   > Has done
>   > > Some clever **Linking,**
>   > > > And You've made
>   > > > > Another world
>   > > > > > To suit Yourself?

Or, ..., that You've **remembered**
>   **Who You were,**
>   > When You weren't a "him",
>   > But "her",
>   > > Or, ..., in another lifetime
>   > > Were an Elf!

Oh! Its more
>   Than I can handle! ...!
>   It might even
>   > Be a **scandal,**
>   > > Just to think
>   > > > That **many** "you's"
>   > > > > Were far and near.

And, in fact,
>   There may be more
>   > Of the **"You's"**
>   > > We thought before
>   > > Were enough
>   > > > For Us to handle; ...;
>   > > > > **What a chore!!!**

With so many
    Personalities
        Showing up
           In *new realities*,
                Its no wonder
                    Our world's **said**
                        To be DONE FOR!!!

Since **You are**
    Your own Creator,
      You decide,
        Both now, and later,
          What You want to be, ...,
            ..., And You'll **know**
              The reason why,

Then, in everything
    You **ARE**
      There is a lesson
        From afar
          That is helping
            The **REAL YOU**
              To bloom, ...,
                ..., **Oh, my!!!**

There's a **copy** of **"Me"**
    Somewhere, ...,
      Let us hope
        It isn't **"malware"**
          That is spreading
            Vicious rumors
              Round the Cosmos.

And I hope
    That "her" physique
        And "her" fortune
           Do not leak
                Requiring wide spread
                    Dispensations
                        Inter vivos!!!

Oh, **please** tell me
    I'm not **"less"**
        Because I can't access
           All those other **"Me's"**
                That travel
                    Here and there,

But, what happens
    When I meet **"them"**?
        And, how ever
           Will I **GREET** **"them"**,
        ..., ...,

                WAIT!

                    I feel **another** poem
                      In the air!! ...

In A Parallel Universe

In a Parallel Universe
    I AM **here**.
        But I'm ALSO
            Located
                Where another is near.

I may have been seen
    At some time
        In some place;
            But I **also** am seen
                Somewhere else, ...
                    ... Out in Space?

Or, perhaps
    I Am wond'ring
        Afar from Earth's base,
            In another dimension,
                Or etheric
                    Kool place!

While I learn
    From my friends
        Who are far from my side,
            That I'm **seen**
                In a place
                    Where some others abide.

Now, **I KNOW**
    That I'm **somewhere**
        For I've seen
            My Own Face!
        And I'm standing
           Right now
                In a well-traveled place.

And **I KNOW**
    That **I AM**
        Where I've seen Me to be, ...,
        And its hard
           To imagine
                There are **TWO** of Me!!

But I've heard
    Without doubt,
        That the others
           Have seen
                Me in some other place, ...,
                  ..., And they're certain . . .
                      That I'm **else**where!
    Alas!!!
        I've passed through
           All Earth's "gas",
              And discovered,
                Time's only
                    A curtain!

Vanessa Conaway Pace
January 7, 2005, Seattle, Washington

In A Parallel Universe

This Is Your Invitation To Create!

Dear Seeker of Those "Deeper Things",

I wish that
    There were **TWO of me,**
        So I could get
            More done, You see,
                And have more time
                    For honey
                        And some tea;

But, somehow
    "Other Me"
        Has not shown up;
            For work, **Or** tea,
        So, I guess I'll have to manage
            (And it may be
                An advantage)
                    With the stuff
                        That is already
                            In my cup.

We **have** everything
    That's needed,
        (And, in fact, the **need's exceeded!**)
            To do everything
                That's in Our heart and mind; ...;

So, ..., just **draw** on
    Those resources,
        (For they're more
            Than earthly horses,)
                And then, just **manifest**
                      The things "**Love**"
                          Has designed.

Now Its YOUR Turn To Be "Creator"!
Put YOUR Thoughts Here, and Read Them Later!

The little book
    That You have made
        Will be a help
            For you to shade
                The Projects
                    That You have in mind.
                  Remember,
                There's more than one
                      Of a kind!

*Now Its YOUR Turn To Be "Creator"!
Put YOUR Thoughts Here, and Read Them Later!*

Now Its YOUR Turn To Be "Creator"!
Put YOUR Thoughts Here, and Read Them Later!

Now Its YOUR Turn To Be "Creator"!
Put YOUR Thoughts Here, and Read Them Later!

Its The ENERGY
You
Send Out

www.pacepublishing.com

Its The **ENERGY** You Send Out
Inspirational Background

> *"If you want to know the secrets of the universe, think in terms of energy, frequency, and vibration."*
> Nikola Tesla

"*I*ts not my fault!" Most every parent on the face of the Earth has heard that at one time or another. "Its not my fault that he fell down. He should'da been watching where my feet were." "Its not my fault we got all muddy. ….. She dared me to wade in there!" "Its not my fault I hit him. Its **his** fault. He made me mad." And on it goes, …, the age old "blame game".

My Mother and Father declared that I had taken that art to a new level one day when I was playing in the yard with my cat, Fluff. Fluff was a wonderful companion in the isolation of country living, and a great mouser for our little farm, but that day she wasn't exactly doing what I wanted her to do. After all, I felt that I was bigger, and smarter than she was, and, therefore, in my little girl power trip, I felt that she should obey what I told her to do!

Not happening! Not that day. She had had enough of playing for that session, and started to go looking for freer stomping grounds. My first reaction was to grab her tail, ..., the part that she had turned to me, ..., and hold her there until she could think things through, and decide that we really were having fun after all. My timing was bad, because just at that moment Mother came out the door, assessed the situation, and scolded **me** for pulling the cat's tail. In self defense I declared that I was **NOT** pulling the cat's tail. I was merely holding on to the cat's tail. It was **the cat** who was doing the pulling!

As you can imagine, it didn't work. The cat went free, and I got the lecture about being kind to animals, and allowing them to be free, and simply enjoying them that way. But my family never let me forget that experience. They held it as a memory of that part of the molding of my personality, and often played that card at family gatherings when people who knew each other well were laughing about the old days. Not much else to do in the West Virginia countryside, ..., before television, and, before some of us left the embrace of those hills. We would miss the "laid-back-ness" of the independent life style that they had chosen by our move to the farm. It was one of those stories that are told and retold; ...; part of a family's history; ...; part of those familiar memories that seem to bond us together as ones who belonged together; ...; ones who have experienced things together, and who are accepting of each other, and who would always be in each other's corner when needed. We were comfortable and secure within our circles.

But, sadly, we left, only to learn that we were to become slaves to the tyranny of the engulfing time and energy demands of our developing technological world.

However, subsequent life experiences began to awaken in me the fact that I was not the only one holding on to the cat's tail, and blaming others for the results. It seemed to be almost a universal Hu-man quality. But, "blame" and "guilt" could not really have been a part of The Original "Love" Design for us Hu-mans. So, where did those ideas come from, how were they so strongly impressed upon us, and, most importantly, how do we get rid of them?

Instinctively I knew that we ALL started out as beings of "Love" aeons ago, but it seems that somewhere down the line the ideas of "blame" and "guilt" were added to our "Love" mix. And, somehow, that "blame" and "guilt" program has been installed on our on-board hard drive, and THAT seems to be eroding those memories of Our True Selves, **which are the ones that should be shaping our perception of Who We ARE! Then we would know and experience the FREEDOM of our truly "guiltless" and "blameless" Selves!!!**

The sneaky little thing that is getting us in trouble is that we have been in the habit of blaming others for things that happen in our lives. But, that was before we understood that we live and move in an established "system" that the Ancient Writings, and modern scientific thought tell us is created out of things that are **NOT!!!**

How can that be??? It seems real enough in our experience that we are physical Beings that are seeing, touching, hearing, and smelling physical things, so, how can it be that they are created out of things that are **NOT???**

A little study of those Ancient Writings, and the new scientific thought shows that everything is created out of the ENERGIES released by our thoughts, feelings, and emotions. In my readings I see that Wisdom Keepers throughout all Ages, and all walks of life, and Nobel Prize winning scientists alike have known that all things that exist are created from things (like thoughts, feelings, and emotions) that are "unseen". We are cautioned that, "Where the mind goes, the body goes", or, in scientific lingo, everything is energy (as Nikola Tesla tells us in the opening quote of this chapter), and everything vibrates. So, what is the SOURCE of that energy?

Oh, dear! Its **"Us"** again! **We're IT!** We **ARE** the dynamo that creates the ENERGY that shapes the world that We live in!

Its just like me and the cat. The feelings that I was putting out were causing the cat to pull away. That force is called ENERGY!

Is the ENERGY that we are putting out attracting the cat, controlling the cat, making life good for the cat, using the cat for our own purposes, or, are we even thinking about the cat, which would really be a good idea, since the ENERGY that is being put out is affecting everything around us, and it is creating the predictable response that is returned back to its sender. Then We can decide whether the ECHO that we are getting back is something that we want, or, whether our ECHOES are showing us that we need to change our thoughts, feelings, or emotions in order to initiate some ECHOES that are more to our liking!!

So, let me think: Who is responsible for **(and can, therefore, change)** the ENERGY that we are getting back???

OUCH! Now I do feel a poem coming on.

Its The **ENERGY** You Send Out

Its the **ENERGY**
  You send out
    That **creates**
      The thing desired.

Its the **ENERGY**
  You send out
    That's **the Force**
      With which
        Its **FIRED!**

Its the **ENERGY**
  You send out
    That will **change**
      The dark
        To **LIGHT,**

Its the **ENERGY**
  You send out
    That **brings** "Vision"
      Into "Sight"!

Its the **ENERGY**
  You send out
    That will loosen
      Stuff that's "mired".

Its the **ENERGY**
    You send out
        That **enlivens**
            Stuff that's **"tired"**.

Its the **ENERGY**
    You send out
        That will **set**
            The "wrongs"
                To **"RIGHTS"**.

Its the **ENERGY**
    You send out
        That will
            Manifest
                Your **"Might"**.

Its the **ENERGY**
    You send out
        That will **"Trump"**
            The "Ace" that's played.

Its the **ENERGY**
    You send out
        That will **"Right"**
            Mistakes *We've made.*

Its the **ENERGY**
>You send out
>>That **cancel**
>>>Foolish thoughts.

Its the **ENERGY**
>You send out
>>That **establishes**
>>>The "**oughts**".

Its the **ENERGY**
>You send out
>>That will **make**
>>>The "ugly" fade.

Its the **ENERGY**
>You send out
>>That **marks all accounts**
>>>As "**PAID**"!!

Its the **ENERGY**
>You send out
>>That **determines**
>>>What You've wrought...

Whether "LOVE", ..., Or "HATE",
>Your **ENERGY**
>>Determines what You've bought!!!

Yes!!! Its the **ENERGY**
> *You send out*
>> *That* **turns** *"Dreams"*
>>> *Into "Designs".*

Its the **ENERGY**
> *You send out*
>> *That* **sends** *"wires"*
>>> *To your "aligns".*

Its the **ENERGY**
> *You send out*
>> *That "attracts"*
>>> *A good position.*

Or, the **ENERGY**
> *You send out*
>> *Might require*
>>> *A new rendition!*

For, the **ENERGY**
> *You send out*
>> *Without thinking*
>>> *Could malign; . . .*

> *Which would make*
>> *You* **reconsider**,
>>> *And send something*
>>>> *More* **"benign"**.

Yes!!! The **ENERGY**
    You send out
        *Will **determine***
            Your condition.

    Just remember,
        *You can **change** it*
            By an act
                Of Your volition!!!

For, the **ENERGY**
    You send out
        *Is **connected***
            To The Vine,

    That determines
        All our futures, ...,
            Surely Yours,
                And truly Mine.

KNOW! The **ENERGY**
    You send out
        With the strength
            Of Your ambition,

        *Will **cause** Light*
        To shape
            Into the form
                That Your Words
                      Gave permission!!

LOVE The **ENERGY**
  You send out.
    Truly let
      Your LOVE LIGHT
        Shine!

  And the **ENERGY**
    You send out
      Will ***make***
        Something
          Quite Divine!!!

But, the **ENERGY**
  You *send out*
    In a ***Negative***
      Emission

  Gives a power to
    UNWANTED things
      That ***causes***
        Quick Ignition.

So, just SMARTEN UP!
    And **choose** to *Love*,
        Yes!! Make that
            Great transition.

Rise up!

    ASCEND!

        Make LOVE your goal.

            And join

EARTH'S NEW CONDITION!!!!!!!!

                      Vanessa Conaway Pace
              November 6, 2006, Seattle, Washington

www.pacepublishing.com

Its The ENERGY You Send Out

> This Is Your Invitation To Create!

Dear Seeker of Those "Deeper Things",

Put your **thoughts here**,
 Then **add**
  *The "****Energy****" ingredient*
   That **causes plans**
    To come to **life**
     In manners
      Quite expedient.

You'll find
 That one small action **Starts**
  The process of creation,
   So, ..., till the soil, ...,
    ..., And plant the seed, ...,
     And **start**
      Your dream's
       Gestation!

Now Its YOUR Turn To Be "Creator"!
Put YOUR Thoughts Here, and Read Them Later!

It's time to take
    Some ACTION now,
        And you will see
            RESULTS, ...,
                ..., And How!!!

*Now Its YOUR Turn To Be "Creator"!
Put YOUR Thoughts Here, and Read Them Later!*

Now Its YOUR Turn To Be "Creator"!
Put YOUR Thoughts Here, and Read Them Later!

Now Its YOUR Turn To Be "Creator"!
Put YOUR Thoughts Here, and Read Them Later!

No Meaning???

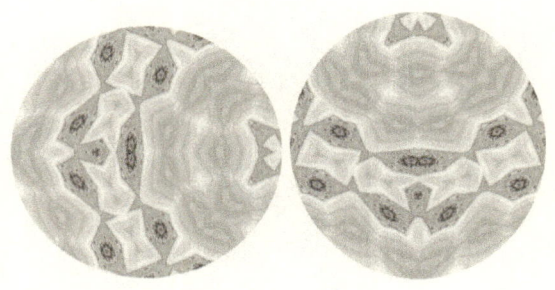

www.pacepublishing.com

No Meaning???
Inspirational Background

It seems that our fitness-conscious society has gone mad these days with one new diet after another, each advertised to be the magic potion that will guarantee that, if we will only follow their formula (and pay their price) we will easily morph into the desired physical dimensions, perform at the promised Olympic levels of streamlined proficiency, and develop muscles that the Greek art portrays as "natural" for the human physique. One pound over the legal limit of "someone's" chart of desirable weights per inch of height brings out the long accusing finger of the "fat" police...,

*Author, Susan Powter brings some sanity to that particular brand of terrorism in her hysteria-diffusing book entitled "Stop the Insanity". She effectively puts the "fat" police out of business and attempts to restore some common sense and practicality into the hyper-physical fitness craze that keeps society busy running to the gym to work out on machines, ..., an effort that **produces** nothing but the compulsion to come back tomorrow and pump more iron, ..., so they can do it again the next day.*

Farmers, like we were, on the other hand, who are busy getting all the exercise they need by the daily use of their muscles to produce the crops they need for health and vitality, would wonder at such a flagrant waste of the treasured energy they need to create something useful. My Father laughed at such a waste of treasured manpower; ...; "Vanessa, go out there in the garden and dig out some weeds. You'll get all the exercise you need, and you will have something to show for it in the end." There is something very logical and satisfying about that kind of self-sufficiency.

I was never "fat" as a child. ... One could have said that I was "corn fed", and healthy, but never "fat". Oh, yes, I always wanted to be a little leaner, a little less "athletic looking", maybe even a little more "helpless delicate feminine looking", but then, those physical frames would not have equipped me for my role in life as a "farm girl". There were chickens to take care of, and their heavy water and feed to haul. And, there was plowing to be done, ground to be prepared for planting, and natural fertilizers to muscle out to the fields so that we could have bigger and more nutritious crops to eat and sell. And then, because we did such a good job of all of that, there were the copious fruits and vegetables that had to be picked and carried up those West Virginia Hills, and then either canned for our winter's nutrition, or hustled off to our many waiting and faithful customers.

Any way you cut it, it was heavy, continuous, and emotionally, intellectually, socially, and physically demanding work. Days were long. The sun was hot. The sunburns hurt. The blisters, insect bites and bee stings persisted. But it was our life. And we were united as a family, enjoying our bounty, and **happy**. ...

Well, **YES**, I was **happy**, except for that gnawing feeling down inside. Somehow, even though I had not been there, and seen it with my own eyes, and experienced it with my own senses, *I KNEW* that there had to be more to life than our little four acres, and the limited number of locals that comprised our social life, and, the simple mountain melodies (beautiful as they are), and the country bands that played for Saturday night square dances. **THERE HAD TO BE MORE.**

Composer Carlisle Floyd brilliantly captured my yearnings in his folk opera entitled "**Susannah**". His leading lady, Susannah Polk, understood me. We were kindred spirits; ...; mountain girls, being swallowed up by irreplaceable folks that we loved, and the slow-paced surroundings that spawned us. On the one hand, the majestic mountains protected us from the unknowns of the outside world, but, on the other hand, they became an imposing citadel that limited our view of worlds that we could not even imagine. But they also provided us no opportunities to spread our wings and fly into the arms of our chosen destinies.

After years of Voice training I later got to sing Susannah's poignant aria entitled "Ain't It A Pretty Night", which was sung to her friend, Little Bat. The words hit a little too close to home for me, and often it was difficult to finish. One portion was particularly difficult.

A good composer can often paint the inner feelings of a character with a single note, or a descriptive set of notes, and Carlyle Floyd brilliantly accomplishes that with the first six notes of the aria. Susannah is longingly looking up at the stars, and she instinctively knows that they are looking down on far-away cities where life is very different from her earth-bound home deep in the shadows of the mountains. Nights there are beautiful, but her vista is small, and Floyd paints the heart tone of her lonely feelings of isolation with the use of the unresolved interval of a major seventh.

    The human ear is satisfied when a melody line jumps from the root note of a musical scale up to its octave note, but when the melodic line only reaches to the seventh note of the octave our musical sense requires that the seventh note resolve either upward, to the completion of the octave, or downward to the sixth step of the musical scale, which has a warm, haunting sound. He chose the latter resolution, and so, both singer and audience feel the incompleteness of Susannah's life as she asks the rhetorical question, "Ain't it a pretty night".

    Susannah is doing what us isolated farm folk have done for aeons; she is gazing into the night sky, and knowing that those stars up there can see things in the distant big cities that she has never seen. And she wonders what its like beyond them mountains. Our only knowledge of the mysterious *people out there came from the pictures we saw in the mail order catalogs!*

Susannah, like me, **had** to go exploring. The adventure of Life could not be spent dusty, and dirty, and tired in the tomato patch! She, like me, aimed to see all those tall buildings, and the city lights, and longed to **BE** one of those city folks. ...,

Somebody please pull the curtain before the audience realizes the Soprano is singing her own life's story, and those tears are not just a good actress singing her part well. Why must life be so filled with those bittersweet experiences? But, something inside of us knows the poignancy of leaving home.

As is often the case when we take those breathtaking leaps into the future, I had no way of knowing the price of following a dream. Again, Carlyle Floyd's Susannah spoke eloquently when she began to wonder if she could get lonesome for the home she had known, and for the familiar sounds and smells and pastoral scenes of nature, and for the security of the beautiful mountains. It was all rolled up in that security blanket called "home".

Then we comfort ourselves with the false hope that we can always go back "home". Susannah hopes, and numbs the anticipated pain of separation with the opiate thought that the valley that she so loved would be there, waiting, should homesickness drive her back there after she had seen what was beyond those mountains.

But, somehow Susannah, and all of us who have **had** to spread our wings and fly, have failed to reckon with the unrelenting fact that when the eagle breaks free of the birth nest, nature's plan is for us to grow. And, even if we do return to the nest, it will be in a different position, and with a new perspective on life, because our eyes have beheld another, more expanded world, and that colors our vision of the nest.

But, I digress! "Fat" was not part of the active, healthy life-style of us farm folk! But WHY? Considering that we ate all that we wanted, and more, of southern fried chicken, mashed potatoes with yummy freshly churned butter and gravy, juicy vine ripened tomatoes with lots of mayonnaise, home-made bread or biscuits with that wonderful butter and still warm home-made jam, freshly pulled corn on the cob with butter dripping from our chins, followed by strawberry/raspberry/peach/or whatever-else-was-in-season shortcake (with heavy whipped cream freshly milked from the cow!), or chocolate cake with piles of fudge icing. WHY didn't we get "fat"?

I suspect that the answer lies in our EXPECTATIONS. We didn't **expect** to get "fat". We didn't think our wonderful bounty would harm us. We **expected** that it would make us healthy and strong, and that we would have the energy to perform the tasks at hand. We simply went outside and worked (or played) it off, and by the time we came in we were legitimately hungry for more!

Quantum Physics teaches us that **"the observer changes the observed"**. We simply lived by a different yardstick, and we got what we were believing for. If we had thought that our normal repast would harm us, it would have! As we learned elsewhere in this book, in the poem **"FOCUS"**, our minds are so powerful that they create what we are thinking about. We **"FOCUS"**ed on a different thought, and, therefore, we created a different outcome. "Elementary, my Dear Watson"!! Today, we are told, "Don't eat this; it will make you "fat"; "Don't eat that; it will cause _____". And, what do you know, it DOES, simply because great minds got into agreement over it!

Moderation and Wisdom in all things, of course. But, if we ARE the powerful creative Beings that we are learning that we ARE, then it seems reasonable that We can intelligently decide what outcomes We want, spend some energy *"FOCUS"*ing on that desire, and then, enjoy Our harvest!!!

You mean I can change the caloric count of my food! And, thereby, recalibrate its "fat"-generating qualities?!!!

I will point you to an article that Michelle Walling posted to the In5D.com website on December 18, 2015. She credits the source of http://howtoexitthematrix.com/2015/12/18/reality-doesnt-exist-until-we-measure-it-quantum-experiment-confirms/ . The title says it all: "Reality Doesn't Exist Until We Measure It, Quantum Experiment Confirms".

YAHOO!!! That says that if I don't **count** the calories, then **they don't exist**, ..., and I can get back to my childhood enjoyment of yummy foods, and never count the cost, and never wear them on unfortunate locations in my body!!!

Oh, YES!!! I DO hear a poem coming on!!!

No Meaning???

Time has no meaning,
    Of that we are sure; ...;
        These days we can't tell
           If an hour,
               Or more.

So, if *"Time"*
    Has no meaning,
        Let Us get one thing straight, ...,
           If those minutes
               Don't count,
                   Let Us talk about
                      "Weight".

If the **clock** doesn't matter
    In this Earth-bound dimension,
        Do the **scales**
           Also fall
               In that line of declension???

If the *"absolute"*
    We've always
        Reckoned as *"Time"*
           Has been swallowed
               In space-speak,
                   Scales ain't
                        Worth a dime!!!!

So, bring on the Chocolate,
    Cookies, and Cake,
        Potatoes **WITH TRIMMINGS**,
      And let's all partake!

No more
    Of the bondage
        Of "calories" fear;
            Just grab the lasagna,
                And bring some
                      Right here!

We'll dine
    Without thinking
        Of what it might mean
            If we overate mildly; ...;
                Bring deserts
                      Thought obscene!

We'll eat
    What We want!!!
        (We might even get healthy!)
        And We won't
            Have to feel
                Its a "sin",
                      Or be stealthy!

*We are **FREE***
    Of the "boxes"
        We put Ourselves in.
            In this Age
                Love won't Limit;
LET THE PARTY BEGIN!!!!!!!

                      Vanessa Conaway Pace
                January 1, 2007, Seattle, Washington

No Meaning???

> **This Is Your Invitation To Create!**

      Dear Seeker of Those "Deeper Things",

There **is** no limit
    To the **size** and **shape**
        Of dreams You can design. ….
            Whatever **You**
                Can conjure up
                    Is **sure**
                        To turn out fine,

If only
    You'll **consider**
        That **Your Source**
           Is **NOT** finite.
              Oh, **NOOOO!**
                  It is **NOT** limited
                      By size, or weight,
                        Or height!

It's always been there,
    Saying that,
        "Your wish
            Is My command.",

    So, …, **dare to ask,**
        And soon You'll see
            You'll have
                Your dream
                    In hand!

Now Its YOUR Turn To Be "Creator"!
Put YOUR Thoughts Here, and Read Them Later!

Yes!!!
    Dare to **Dream**,
        And Dare to **PLAN**,
        And then,
            Just **WORK**
                Hard as you can!

Now Its YOUR Turn To Be "Creator"!
Put YOUR Thoughts Here, and Read Them Later!

*Now Its YOUR Turn To Be "Creator"!
Put YOUR Thoughts Here, and Read Them Later!*

Now Its YOUR Turn To Be "Creator"!
Put YOUR Thoughts Here, and Read Them Later!

Our Purpose

www.pacepublishing.com

Our Purpose
Inspirational Background

I really look forward to going out to a nice restaurant and having a special meal with good friends and good conversation. I revel in an opportunity to sit down, be waited on, and sort through all those delicious-looking menu choices. And, there is definitely something to be said for leaving all those dishes for someone else to do! It should be the ultimate dining experience, with the added plus that I don't have to do any of the work!

But, ..., there we are: ...: We've arrived, been graciously seated, enjoyed the luxury of ordering from all those menu choices, settled back with our before-dinner tea and talk,..., And then the meal is served.

The presentation is lovely, and with hopeful anticipation I take the first bite. .... There it is again, ..., That let-down feeling. Its **okay**. It will fill the empty place in my stomach; ..., but, why doesn't it meet the expectations that I had told my palate to prepare for?

*For a long time I thought it was just me being picky about my food. Admittedly, growing up on an "organic" farm had some real advantages. (I thought we used the chicken maneuver for fertilizer because we were too poor to be able to afford all those expensive commercial fertilizers!) On the plus side, it allowed me to know what **REAL** tomatoes and cucumbers and corn tasted like. My well-developed palate can quickly discern when sweetcorn has been off the stock for more than half-an-hour before cooking. Let me assure you,..., its **different** from the taste of some machine picked corn that's been dragged halfway across the country in a hot truck!*

But, could it be that there is something else going on here?

So many times we hear people longingly say how they miss Mother's good home cooking. After I left the farm to go to work in the big city I couldn't wait for the weekends when I could drive across the Appalachian Mountains and beat it home for some of Daddy's fresh vegetables and Mother's home cooking. We would sit around for hours and talk, and eat, and then Mother would load me up with enough leftovers to carry me through the next week of office work and university classes. Yum!

It was later in life when I learned that the "Energy" of the person preparing the food is actually transferred into the food, and, therefore, greatly impacts the taste, quality, and even the molecular structure of the food. Its a bit scary to learn that the "Energy" of an angry person who is preparing the food will affect the "Energy" of the food in much the same way that putting vinegar into milk curdles it!

A delightful lady from Khartoum, Republic of Sudan, Africa, taught me that. I had been terribly sick for three weeks, in bed, and hardly able to take care of my two small children. And, I didn't see any signs of getting any better. She found out about my predicament, and, within a few hours, showed up at my door with fresh eggs, which she scrambled with some heavy whipping cream, and served with fresh strawberries and toast with fresh country butter. Nothing had tasted so good for weeks! I was able to eat it all!

Then the strangest thing happened. She insisted that I go back to bed while she cleared the table, AND the three weeks of dishes. I fell into a peaceful sleep, and, when I awoke there was no sign of the previous sickness! I was full of energy and strength, and, after three miserable weeks, was able to get up and care for myself, my two small children, and the house. How did that happen?

My miracle-working friend then told me that when someone among her people back in Africa would get sick, another person would begin to cook some food, and would consciously infuse healing energy into that food as they were preparing it. Then, with great "Love" they would take the healing-filled food to the friend who had been sick. When that person ate the food they would take in the healing thoughts, and rise up out of their sickness. It had been working for their people for a long long time.

Not long after that I learned that among some "advanced" peoples they would choose the healthiest and wisest among them to do the cooking for the whole group, so that **their** desirable energies would be ingested via the food, and thus the whole group would be advanced to their chef's higher-**"ENERGY"** level. ... Hmmmmmm! ... Maybe we're learning something here!

The other day, in my desperation for some tasty and healthy food, I paid $2.50 for **ONE** small Heritage tomato. ... "Small" meaning that it would fit in the palm of my hand and I could still gently close my fingers halfway over it. This little gem was **NOT** the Hope Diamond, but I figured it would satisfy my craving for some **REAL** food for a while.

Granted, it was better than the watery hothouse tomatoes we so often find in our grocery stores, ..., but, what was missing? What was the difference between my Father's totally delicious, almost solid-all-the-way-through tomatoes and my expensive little dew-drop one? And, why is it that a restaurant-prepared meal somehow doesn't taste the same as Mother's home cooking?

After putting together a lot of things that I have learned and experienced, I think I may have come up with a plausible explanation. It has to do with my African friend's example, ..., and the scientific principles of

"*ENERGY*" *that are explaining how things really work in our everyday world.*

I believe that my expensive commercial organic tomato did not taste the same as my Father's delicious home-grown tomatoes because **his** *were grown with the "Energy" of "Love" and "Caring"* **for ME and OUR FAMILY**. *The "intention" with which we do things determines their ultimate value, ..., and, dare we say that it also even determines our return on investment? Daddy grew his crops as an act of "Love" for his family, and in order to provide for them by using his ability to farm in order to contribute to our greater community. And, in return, we lived well. We worked hard, enjoyed our days, and lived peacefully.*

Yes, I'm sure that the people who grew the tomato I purchased were well-intentioned, higher level people, since they **chose** *to grow the earth-friendly organic crop over the commercially-grown* **for-profit** *crops of large farm conglomerates. But, I submit that the difference in taste and quality is somehow related to the* **intensity** *of the "Love" element that was infused into my Father's tomatoes,* and my African friend's healing food. "**Something**" came out of those people, and into me, that cannot be explained in dollars and cents.

Likewise for my restaurant meal. Mother's home cooking came with an ingredient that could not be measured, or priced, or duplicated: ...: Her intense "**Love**" for me, and, her impassioned hopes for our futures and the great things we would do. All of the thoughts, life experiences, and emotions that made up the unique "**ENERGY**" that I called "Mother" produced a unique "**ENERGY**" that became an actual part of her food, that then became a part of all who ate it. It probably was not even a "conscious" transfer of "Energy" that she did, but, by the unchanging laws of Nature, Mother's "**Love ENERGY**", and Daddy's "**Purposeful Energy**" as he grew the crops, got transferred into the food they prepared. The essences of their lives were all there in every delicious spoonful, and they are forever stored in every molecule of my being.

Most commercial restaurants can't really do that. Well-intentioned as their creators, owners, workers, and suppliers are, they are still an impersonal "commercial endeavor" mostly operating with a "for profit motive", which means that there is a different "intention", which naturally creates a different **"ENERGY"** that is absorbed by the food and subsequently transferred to my palate.

I get it! Restaurant food can never taste like my Mother's cooking, because **theirs** is rooted in **commercialism** and **hers** was rooted in "**Love**". It's just simple physics; the **"ENERGY"** that goes in directly affects the **"ENERGY"** that comes out.

Hmmmmm. You mean that the atmospheres that We live in, and that live within Us, are actually infused with the very "intensions" that We have been putting out all along???!!!

Ohhhh. I think I **DO** feel a poem coming on.....

Our Purpose

"Our Purpose"
    For coming
        From realms far above
           Is to build a great net
                'Round this Earth
                    With Our **Love!**

We've come here
    From lands
        'Cross The Great Crystal Sea
        To embellish
           This realm
                With **Love's**
                    High Frequency!!!

We've come here
    To heal
        All the damage that's done
           When the "loveless"
                Think "THEY"
                    Have the Earth-realm
                  To run.

We can see
    What a mess
        "THEY" have made
           Of Earth's lot;
                While WE
                    Have been dumb
                        To THEIR
                          Sinister plot.

We've forgotten
    Love's shining
        Surely repairs
            All the tears
                In Earth's lining
                    And the garment
                        She wears.

There's **nothing**
    Earth's suffered
        At the hands
            Of dark thoughts
                That can't
                    Be repaired
                        When **WE**
                            Love Her lots!

We do it
    By sending Her
        Thoughts of elation,
            And **by**
                Following those
                    With Our Acts
                        Of CREATION!!!

Whatever
    Your skill,
        Or Your creative bent,
            Get it out,
                Dust it off,
                    And, **by Love**
                        And Intent

Send it out;
    Mark Your spot;
        And Release ALL Your Gifts.
            Give it ALL that You've got
          Never mind
              All those "if's".

When We **THINK**
    On the things
        That are GOOD For Us all,
      We'll make beauty
        From ashes,
          And **REVERSE**
              Their "Great Fall"!!!

But **Love**
    Has awakened
        Our slumbering mind,
            So We **see** the results
                Of that "Loveless-Kind" bind.

And We vaguely Remember
    Through the fog
        Of this Sphere,
           That its **Love**
              That will get Us
                  Our trip out'ta here!!

From Our places
    On Mars, Si-ri-us,
        Or on Venus,
           We saw
              A great need
                For the Love
                    That's between Us

To be carried
    To Earth
        To repair
            All that's rotten,
                ... Its the natural crop
                    That the "**Loveless**"
                        Have gotten!

Its no secret
    To those
        Who have been here before
            That a **Life**
                Without "**Love**"
                    Can be a real bore!

Not to mention
    The pain
        That it causes
            The Earth; ...;
                ...; So, its **HER**
                    That We came for,
                        And **Love's Rebirth**
                            On Earth!!

We have **struggled**
    For eons
        To know
            "**Why I'm here**".
                So, now,
                    Let Me put
                        A wee bug
                            In Your ear...

We're here
> *'Cause We're Light,*
>> *And We're Love, ...*
>>> ***Its Our Nature!***

> *We've just*
>> *Listened to THEM*
>>> *And We've lost*
>>>> *That Great Stature.*

And, We've groveled
> *Down here*
>> *In the pigpen of hate,*
>>> *And, We found out*
>>>> ***The fruit***
>>>>> *Of that slime*
>>>>>> *Ain't that Great!!*

So, Our time
> *In that mess*
>> *Has been quite sufficient*
>>> *To instill a desire*
>>>> *To become*
>>>>> *More **OMNISCIENT!!***

So, **release**
>All that stuff
>>That has darkened
>>>Your LIGHT,
>>>>And **ALLOW**
>>>>>Love to bloom; ...
>>>>>>**It will brighten
>>>>>>Your night.**

And, the **Real You**
>Will Shine
>>With Ascension's
>>>Bright flame.
>>>>It'll burn all the Dross
>>>>>And **reveal**
>>>>>>Your True Name!!

You'll **remember**
>That You saw a need
>>On the Earth,
>>>And **You charted
>>>Your course**
>>>>To come here
>>>>>And give birth

To the "**Love**" Life
>That yields
>>Everything
>>>That Earth needs
>>>>To restore Her
>>>>>To health
>>>>>>At the greatest
>>>>>>>Of speeds.

Yes! *"Our Purpose"* for coming
    From realms
        Far above
            Is to build
                A great net
                    'Round this Earth
                        With Our Love,

And to grow
    To great stature
        And to **BE**
            All We **Are**,
                So We'll shine
                    Through the Ages
                        As a Glorious Star!!!

Vanessa Conaway Pace
November 23, 2007, Seattle, Washington

www.pacepublishing.com

Our Purpose

> ***This Is** **Your**
> **Invitation**
> **To Create!***

Dear Seeker of Those "Deeper Things",

Soooo, Now that you know
    The **real** reason
        Your here,
            It's the time
                That you **MUST**
                    Get Your **rear**
                        Into gear,

And **finish**
    Those projects
        You put on the shelf,
            And bring
                Satisfaction
                    To Your **Truly**
                        Great Self!

And **that**
    Will make room
        For the new ones to come, …,
            And suddenly **Your** life
                Will **not** be
                    Humdrum;

But will **burst**
    With excitement
        Each time You convene,
            And display
                The Creations
                    You brought
                        On the scene!

Now Its YOUR Turn To Be "Creator"!
Put YOUR Thoughts Here, and Read Them Later!

Just take the book
    That You've been creating,...,
        And where You've put
           Your ideas, ...,
              There sitting there, ...,
                  Waiting, ...,

And fuse them with **Love**,
    And the **PLAN**
        Of great **price**,
           And You will decide
              That Your Love
                  Will suffice.

Now Its YOUR Turn To Be "Creator"!
Put YOUR Thoughts Here, and Read Them Later!

Now Its YOUR Turn To Be "Creator"!
Put YOUR Thoughts Here, and Read Them Later!

Now Its YOUR Turn To Be "Creator"!
Put YOUR Thoughts Here, and Read Them Later!

The High Road

www.pacepublishing.com

The High Road
Inspirational Background

An old Scottish aire melodiously taunts that if you take *"The High Road"*, and I take the low road, then I'll be in Scotland before you. To me, as a child singing those old words at the top of my voice, while padding over the hills of our mountain farm in my usually-bare feet, it seemed just natural to think that *"The High Road"* would be the one more desirable, and I determined that I wanted to find **THAT** way for myself in life. Whatever that meant, it just felt right. My little girl instincts told me it was out there, so, now I needed to find out what *"The High Road"* was, where it was, and how I was going to get on it!

Again it was my friends "the Authors", who have often provided the answers that I need, who began to help me determine what *"The High Road"* really meant. I discovered an old book on "The Virtues" that built nicely upon my Mother and Father's teachings about how life could reach higher levels if we would simply live by the principles of **Love**, **Joy**, **Peace**, **Integrity**, etc. Being a product of the practicalities of farm living, I began to understand that *"The High Road"* is so much more than just reading about those Virtues, important as that is. It involves a **lifetime** of **choices**, that are not always lofty and visible, or easy! Sometimes the choices involve practical actions in everyday living, and difficult choices that help us problem-solve in a concrete way.

And then I later learned that the **choices** that we make even affect things **BEYOND** this world, on a UNIVERSAL level. WOW! If that is true, then it is very important for us to learn *"how"* Our influence can be that far reaching, and *"how"* We can fit into that SYSTEM, thereby advancing ourselves as Spiritual Beings having experiences away from "Home"!!! That would truly be life in the fast lane! Hmmmm. Could **THAT** actually be why it is to Our advantage to pay the hard-earned toll to travel on **"The High Road"** of Our unending life?

Childhood experiences permanently embed themselves in Us, and, for better or for worse, they contribute greatly to the qualities that We wear in later life. Then it happens that, once We consciously discover those qualities, we get to **choose** whether We want to embrace them for their appreciated value in Our lives, or, begin to blame those who were there during those early experiences for our later struggles.

The good news is that those qualities that We discover in Ourselves **can** be changed, …, **when** We have a mind to change them. But, the "level" of the road that We must travel to bring Us to the point of that decision, and the pathway to that change, can be quite bumpy.

"The High Road" IS bumpy, and, I believe that it is bumpy for a purpose. It forces Us to **inflate our inner tires** so that We can have a more comfortable ride.

My Father used to drive Us in Our antique Ford over the rut-filled back country roads of West Virginia. The ride was bumpy, but it was the only way to get from "here" to "there" without walking, which could take hours! Smooth paved roads were not all that plentiful in our neck of the woods.

I remember one day when we were driving back in the holler to see our friends who lived **after** the end of the dirt road. It had rained very hard the day before, and, not only were the old ruts in the mud making our trip bumpy, but, earlier in the afternoon, someone had chosen to cut new ruts with their tires, and the mess that they made was causing our car to be thrown around uncontrollably. All too often we found ourselves looking down into the ravine from the unprotected edge of the dirt road. It was a scary experience for all of us. But Daddy found a better way to navigate through that dangerous situation.

As a little girl in the back seat I kept wondering why Daddy didn't just drive in the **old** ruts, like he always seemed to do. But this time he put our narrow tires up on the plateau of the old ruts, and drove on **top** of them. As usual, I had to know **why** he was doing that. He patiently explained that if We were to drive down in the low ruts there were exposed, and even worse, sometimes **hidden** rocks with sharp edges that would tear up the tires, or jut up and break the axle, and then we'd really be stuck. (They didn't put many garages out there in the boonies!!!) Or, sometimes the ruts were so deep that the bottom of the car would drag on them, tearing out brake and gas lines, or, worse yet, lifting the tires clear up off the ground. Can't go very far that way!! So, his solution was to drive up on

top of all of the dangers, put his narrow tires on the muddy crests of the ruts, thus mashing the tall ruts down, and, thus somewhat leveling the entire road.

And then, he added another explanation that has stuck with me through the years. We didn't have a lot of heavy equipment that could come in there and flatten out the road for all of us. His reasoning for driving up on the **top** of the ruts was so that our tires would press down the mountainous ruts, **and thereby begin to level the rest of the road.** And, he reasoned that if **everyone** who drove that road would do the same then we could all ride comfortably. **In his practical way, Daddy had chosen "The High Road" that considers the well-being of others.** He made life a little easier and safer for everyone.

It was such a simple, and yet practical way of choosing "**The High Road**" in life. And his actions embedded that principle in me. Even now, as I do my everyday travels, I still drive on the **edges** of the ruts, in order to smooth out our roadways for everyone's safety and comfort! It only took a few tires to cut those ruts, and it will only take a few tires to smooth them out!!

I'm sure we can all think of examples where someone's choice of taking **"The High Road"** has made a difference in our own lives, and in the lives of others.

Who wouldn't want to live "The High Road"??!! The higher we personally, and collectively, live, the more ruts in our Earth we will smooth out, and the higher level of life we will create for ourselves and for others. We can do it **together**! We can **create "The High Road"** amongst the struggles of life, and that will result in an even a higher level of life while we are on this Planet, and, that will result in a higher level of life for us when we arrive at the next one! Now **that's** just plain good old West Virginia logic!!

Oh, my! I sure do feel a poem coming on, and its **singing** itself to that old Scottish aire!!!

The High Road

Sung to the tune of an old Scottish Aire

When You take
    "The High Road"
        It never is
            A *"super"* road
                Where You see the way
                    Long before You;

It jumps and it dives
        And it switches
             Side to side; ...
                You can know
                    That the ride
                        Will not bore You!!!

One step up
    "The High Road"
        Will lead You
            To **The Light,** You know;
                The Kings' Highway
                    Opens before You.

It spirals up **The Light,**
        And diffuses darkest night,
            Where there ain't nothin' good
            Waitin' for You!

There's Friends on
  "The High Road"
    To take You to
      The Mother Load,
        'Cause they've walked
         "The High Road"
          Before You.

They've **learned**
  All the tricks,
    And they'll tell You
      How to fix
       All the things
        That have started
         To bore You!

Just **STAY**
  On *"The High Road"*;
    Forget about
      The low road;
       And **You'll see**
        The New World
         Before you.

  Enjoy sweet release
    As You see Your world
      In **Peace,**
       For the ***dawnin'***
        Of The Age
         Is upon You!

There's **Love**
    On *"The High Road"*;
        Its ***better***
            Than the low road;
              And **Love**
                  Makes the World bloom
                    In ***Beauty!!***

It ***heals*** all the wounds,
    And it makes
        The darkness **Light**;
            For The **Love**
              That mends the World
                Is within **You!**

We're ***free***
    On *"The High Road"*;
        There's ***bondage***
            On the low road;
                Up high there is free
                    Sunny weather;

Forgiveness for Me,
    And forgiveness
        For You, too;
            And We'll all walk
                "The High Road"
                    Together.

If You take
> **The High Way**
>> You'll tap into
>>> The DNA,
>>>> And **know**
>>>>> All of what's gone
>>>>>> Before You.

You'll **know**
> **All that's True,**
>> And the Joy
>>> That waits for **You,**
>>>> And the **Glory**
>>>>> That is **there**
>>>>>> **Waiting for You!**

Vanessa Conaway Pace
June 2003, Seattle, Washington

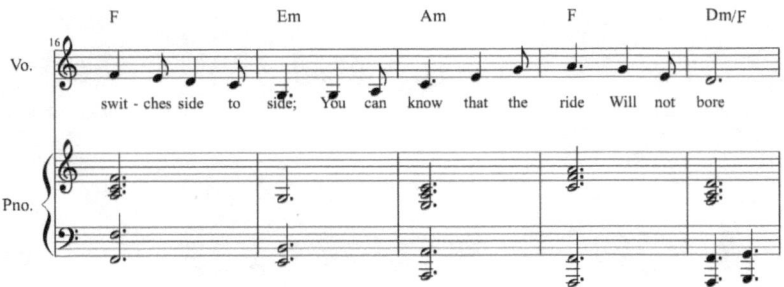
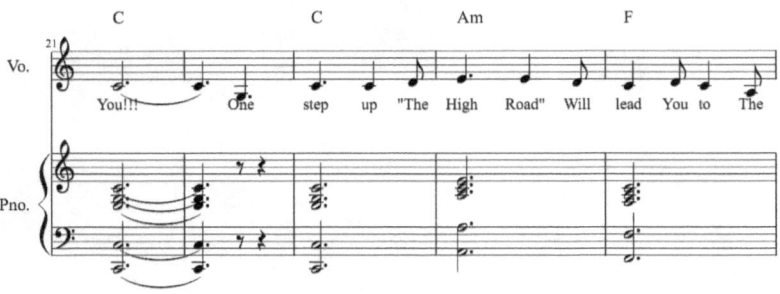
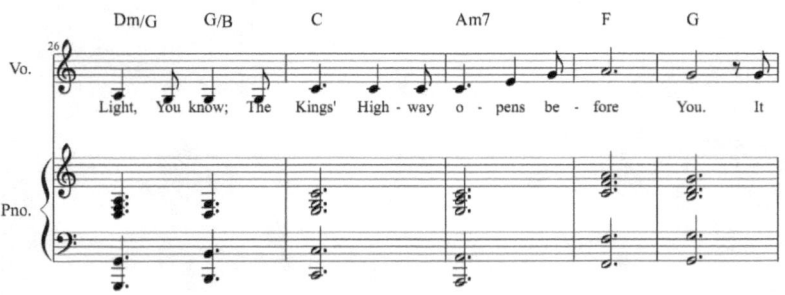

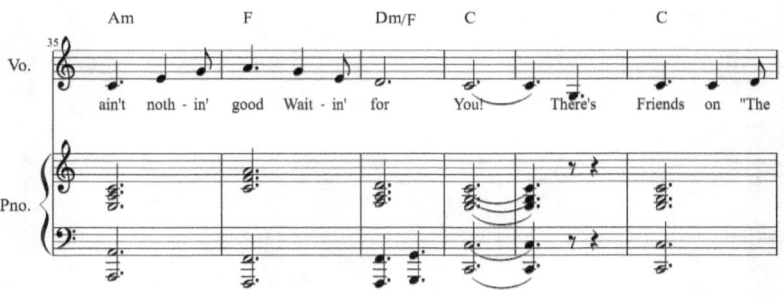

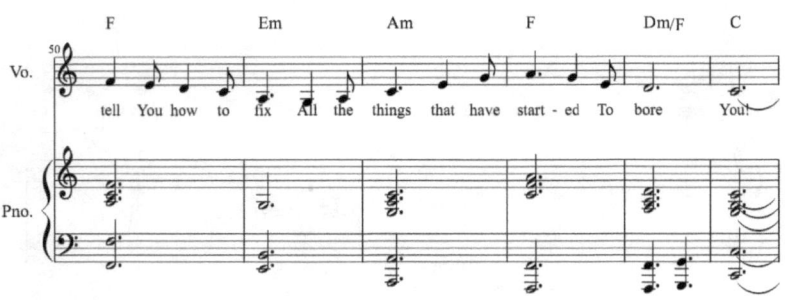

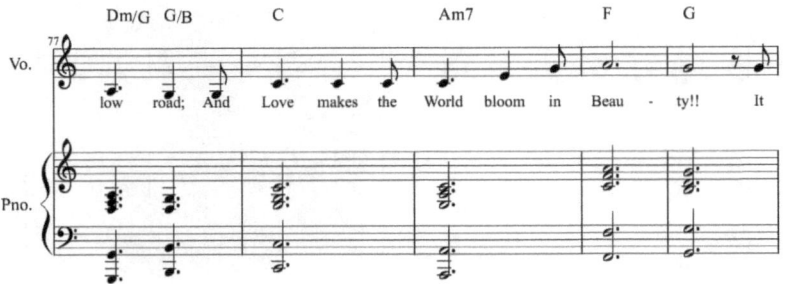
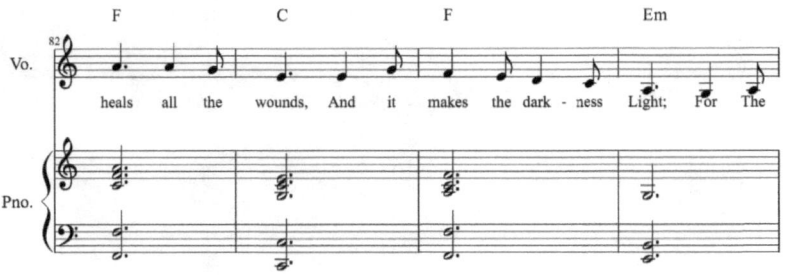

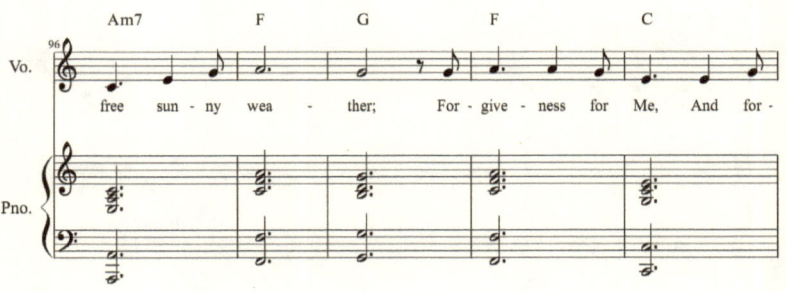

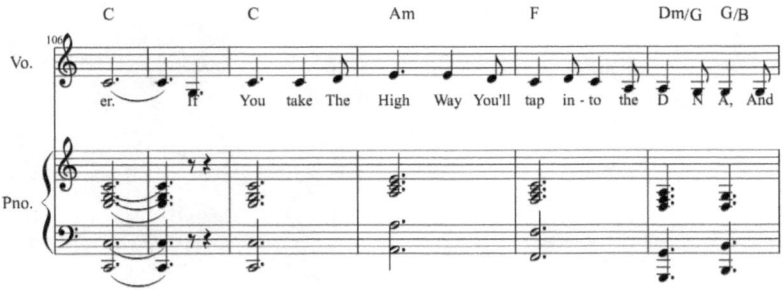

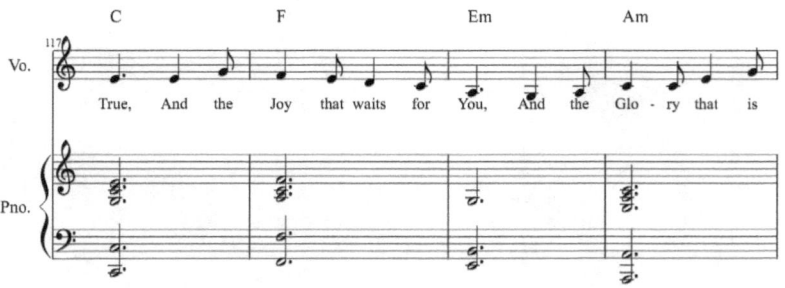

www.pacepublishing.com

The High Road

This Is Your Invitation To Create!

Dear Seeker of Those "Deeper Things",

The **Road** that You take
    Has brought You
        To "**Here**"; ...;
            But, ..., please also
                Remember
                    That **there's**
                        Another Road
                          Near.

And You can make **choices**
    That determine
        Your outcome; ...;
            Just remember
                That **Greatness**
                    Is not something
                        You're **far** from.

Soooooo,
    Please
        Choose the road
            That **isn't so prickly,**
                And follow Your dreams
                    There,
                        So you'll arrive
                            Quickly!!!

Now Its YOUR Turn To Be "Creator"!
Put YOUR Thoughts Here, and Read Them Later!

Just keep on working
    On the book
        You have begun,
            And soon You will see
                *There is a **High Way***
                    To run, ...,
            *A **better way** calling*
                *That makes Your Life **FUN**!*

So, now, just remember
    *To **work** in your book,*
        And put Your ideas down
            There where You'll look;
                And then You will hasten
                    *To walk the **High Way***
            To complete
                All those projects
                    You wanted today!

*Now Its YOUR Turn To Be "Creator"!
Put YOUR Thoughts Here, and Read Them Later!*

Now Its YOUR Turn To Be "Creator"!
Put YOUR Thoughts Here, and Read Them Later!

Now Its YOUR Turn To Be "Creator"!
Put YOUR Thoughts Here, and Read Them Later!

The Flow of Love

www.pacepublishing.com

The Flow Of Love
Inspirational Background

> *"If we want our species to survive,*
> *if we are to find meaning in life,*
> *if we want to save the world*
> *and every sentient being that inhabits it,*
> ***love the is the one and only answer.***"
> *Albert Einstein*

I once heard a Speaker in a large convention say that the problems of this world could have all been over at any time that enough of Us agreed together on how We wanted things to be! That revelation brought up several emotions in me: (1) The deepening sense of awe at the idea that We actually **have** *the innate authority and ability to accomplish such a thing; (2) the unbridled excitement of, if that is really true, "Then let me in the game, Coach!" ; (3) the fear of all of the changes that would bring to my known patterns of existence; and, (4) a sudden rush of what We will call "righteous indignation" at the people who have gone before me that have not used their innate abilities to create that better world so that We could have had a better time of it in this generation!*

After years of seeking the development of "me", I began to realize that there had to be a higher purpose in "life", so, I dared to ask the ultimate question of, "What is TRUTH?" When We ask a question We can be certain that the answer will come. When they came I hungrily followed every "lead" and rabbit trail that my instincts and open mind sniffed out. Consequently I began to understand the "reasons" that the convention Speaker was right.

His bold statement brought to light the realization that there is within each of Us an endless potential for personal development, and that when We develop Ourselves it then overflows into Our environment, to those around Us, and on into all of Creation. We are all connected to the Source of that "potential". We just have to realize that We **have** that connection, that We **have** the right to use it, and that we must nurture it. For example, Nature shows us how this principle works. Consider the apple at the end of a branch that has become disconnected from the rest of the apple tree. For a while it still looks like it's original design, but there's no nourishing "flow" from its Source. Without that healthy connection to its food source nobody will pick it because it is obviously withering up from malnutrition. It can't put out enough energy to attract anything that wasn't designed to remove its *fruitless decay from the landscape. Then it can be given another chance in Nature's recycle system. The apple's lost connection to its Source stopped its potential for its own development, and literally affected the entire Field of "Life".*

The logical question then becomes, "What was the "substance" that was "flowing" to (and from) that apple tree that was necessary to sustain not only the apple's life, but everything that, in turn, the apple would nourish? Enter the above quote from what our collective history has recognized as one of our great "thinkers". It seems that our great "scientific thinker" also had another side to him that is not often recognized by what we have been trained to call "Science". We are told that our great "scientific thinker" wrote some 1,400 letters which he left to his daughter Lieserl, with orders not to publish their contents until two decades after his death. So, it is reported that in the late 1980s' Einstein's daughter donated those letters to the Hebrew University.

One part of those letters indicated that Einstein felt that no one understood him when he proposed his famous theory of relativity, and by the same token he would expect that the world would also misunderstand his thoughts about love. Therefore, it is said that he asked his daughter to hold on to those particular letters until our society is advanced enough to accept the radical ideas about love that he was going to present in them.

A quick look at history will show us that at the time that our "scientific thinker" was writing this message our world was at war. The governing powers were using the very scientific advancements that our "scientific thinker" so well understood and created, to destroy, rather than to **build**, and it seems that our "scientific thinker" discerned that a world that would use his precious scientific truths to harm others was not worthy to know the creative, nourishing, generative "force" that was behind his scientific theories.

The www.In5D.com website article of March 5, 2016, that I was reading continues with Einstein's thoughts concerning an immensely powerful force that current science could not explain. He reckoned that the universal force called "Love" governed all other forces, and that it was the force behind any phenomena operating in the universe. And, he further surmises that "Love" is Light that shines in those who operate by its principles. He espouses that "Love" is the gravitational force that causes one person to be attracted to another. He even goes so far in that letter to equate "God" with "Love"!

And then, it is reported that our "scientific thinker" offers a most welcome hope for humanity by declaring that each of Us has **within us** the power to generate that "Love"!!!

Oh, it is definitely time to turn cartwheels and rejoice! We, who have so long longed for "Love", and the "feeling" of "Love", and the liberating confidence that we are safely embraced by the Brotherhood of Man, are actually **"containers"** of this all powerful "force", and can, therefore, release it from **within** Us! In fact, we **ARE** that "force" in our world!!!

Oh, I **DO** feel a poem flowing through!........

ADDENDUM

Authors Note: *After writing the above "Inspirational Background" for the following poem,* **"The Flow Of Love"***, I was searching for the contact information for the website in which I first saw the article that quoted Einstein's letters to his daughter, Lieserl. I encountered some disturbing news. Some on the Internet were questioning the origin of the letters, claiming family circumstances that would have precluded their publication. Others, who were in responsible positions as curators of other Einstein letters were claiming that these letters to his daughter were not written in the typical Einstein style, and therefore, could not be attributed to his pen. And, the debate raged on.*

The open discussion format of our World Wide Web is one of Earth's greatest "wonders" where all are equally free to express their ideas. We can share our own insights around the world, and learn from the rich experiences of each other. While following the thread of the Einstein letters debate I found within the questionings of the scientific and skeptical minds, an interesting observation by **one** *who had searched a little deeper, and was relying on the musings of a mind that is tempered by the heart, rather than programmed intellectuality. That person suggested that perhaps these letters had been written by someone who had discovered universal truths, and was desperate to share those Truths with all who would receive them, ..., but instinctively knew that the mentality of much of our current media-trained civilization would not accept such truths unless those "pearls of Wisdom" could be attributed to someone who was recognized as an "expert" or "genius" by that society.*

I was saddened by the realization that he was probably right. Somewhere along the line humanity seems to have been told that only those with a certain "fame" can possibly know Truth, ..., and the rest must simply unquestioningly follow that chosen one's thoughts.

Here, the childlike heart of the "Poet" greets you, my fellow traveler, and encourages you to be like the observer mentioned above, who would dare do to **follow his heart** in this process of discerning the value of the thoughts that had been attributed to Einstein. The childlike heart of the "Poet" sees the mysteries of history in the tiny rings of the tree, sees the wonders of the universe encoded in a magnified gemstone, and sees intuitively into the happenings on our planet while viewing the scientific results of core borings of the earth.

We are Living Soul Extensions of The Source of All That Is, so We certainly have within Us all that is necessary to enable each of Us to follow our own instincts, and We can look at the things that have been attributed to our recognized scientific "genius", and **We can decide life's issues for ourselves, by following our own heart.** That is the innate genius of us Living Souls! Our on-board computers (minds) already know "Truth", and can spot it a mile away! Each of Us can be our own "Genius"!!!

Perhaps Einstein's "genius" was not just formulating thoughts in his "mind", but that he could bring them through his heart, and thereby come closer to the "Truth".

In my "poetic" view, the debate of the issue doesn't really matter. What matters is that his thoughts on "Love" are inspirational, and reflecting on them encourages me to loftier ideals about **"The Flow Of Love"**.

www.pacepublishing.com

The Flow of Love

When *"**The FLOW Of Love**"*
    Is thwarted,
        You will find
            A process started
                That will lead You
                    Down a lonely,
                        Darkened path.

When **Love's** circulation's
    Turned off,
        You will find Your crop's
           Been burned off,
              And **Your Life**
                  Has stopped creating, ...,
                    Do the math!!!

Where You once
    Had **care for others,**
        Now, when given
           All Your druthers,
        You'd prefer
           To hide within
                Your own Life's pain.

When, the very
    Act of **caring**
        Was the thing
           That gave an airing
              To the **Real You,**
                And allowed
                  Your Soul
                    To gain.

When the *flow of Life's*
    Diverted,
        All that's left
        Is what's
            Been "hurted",
                And Life's **Well** within
                    Has suddenly
                        Gone dry.

When Life's River
    Stops its flowing,
        You will find within
            A knowing
                That if You
                    Don't *fast*
                        Start rowing
                            You will die.

There's a certain part
    That wants to
        Cash your chips in,
            But **that**
                You can't do,
                    'Cause the system
                        Works unflinchingly
                            This way:

That "diversion"
    You created
        When Your Great Life Plan
        Was stated
            Was to make You grow,
                And **CHOOSE**
                      Another way!

So, the moral
    Of the story
        Is to find
           A deeper Glory
              In Yourself,
                  And then,
                      Develop it
                          Tout suite.

For, those **riches**
    Deep within You
        Cannot easily
           Begin to
                Make Life **richer**
                    'Til their mining
                        Is complete.

KNOW the **Beauty**
    That's within You,
        And is stored
           In every sinew,
               Is so needed
                   By this world
                       To which We came,

That,
    Without You
        We can't make it!

So, if you'll kindly fake it,
    Your own Will
        Will help you make it,
           And, **together,**
               We can **WIN**
                   This Earthly game!

Lay aside
> That Life that's sloven;
>> **Put some Lovin'**
>>> **In Your oven,**
>>>> And reach out
>>>>> With what **You ARE**
>>>>>> To just a few.

You'll discover
> Something wondrous,
>> And, perhaps
>>> A little humorous,
>>>> That,.....
>>>>> In seeing them,
>>>>>> You're really
>>>>>>> Seeing You!!!

Its enough
> To make You shudder,
>> And to cause Your tongue
>>> To mutter,
>>>> When You realize
>>>>> We really are
>>>>>> All **One**!

So, the hiding
> That You're doin',
>> **And that brings**
>>> **Your Life to ruin,**
>>>> Even interrupts
>>>>> Love's flow
>>>>>> Upon The Sun.

Well, If all of Life's connected,
    Then,
        The actions You've elected
            Are affecting
                EVERYTHING
                    In time and space.

And, **EVERYTHING**'s
    A true **unique** thing,
        Soooooo,
           Without the thing
                That You bring
                    There is nothing
                        That can satisfy
                          Your place;

All the Universe
    Is waiting
        For the stuff
           That You're creating,
                And the River's Flow
                Is waiting
                    For Your toe,

So, jump in!
    And let **It** carry
        All the stuff
           That makes you wary,
           And enjoy Life
                In **Love**'s
                    Sparkling River's
                      Flow!!!

                    Vanessa Conaway Pace
            January 1, 2007, Seattle, Washington

www.pacepublishing.com

The Flow of Love

> ### This Is Your Invitation To Create!

Dear Seeker of Those "Deeper Things",

If **You**
    Have been waiting, ...,
        And anticipating, ...,
            That **Life's**
                Gon'na change
                    Without action,

Then, let me assure **You**
    That **Life's**
        Gon'na bore You
            Until **You can**
                CHANGE
                    That distraction!

"Love" has made **You**
    The answer
        To another Soul's need; ...;
            So, **reach out**
                With that **Treasure**
                    Within You
                        With speed,

And discover
    The **Value**
        That **You are**
            To Us, ...,

        And **THAT**
            Will assure You
                That You're
                    A real PLUS!

Now Its YOUR Turn To Be "Creator"!
Put YOUR Thoughts Here, and Read Them Later!

"There Is Greatness Within You"
    *That **needs** to come out,*
        So, take out your book
            *And **ALLOW** Your Downspout*
            To flow out
                With thoughts of these things
                    That You will create,
                And then you will find
                  That You feel
                      Really Great!

Now Its YOUR Turn To Be "Creator"!
Put YOUR Thoughts Here, and Read Them Later!

Now Its YOUR Turn To Be "Creator"!
Put YOUR Thoughts Here, and Read Them Later!

Now Its YOUR Turn To Be "Creator"!
Put YOUR Thoughts Here, and Read Them Later!

There's Greatness Within You

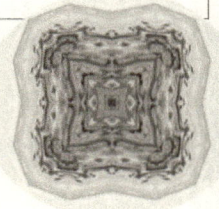

www.pacepublishing.com

There Is Greatness Within You
Inspirational Background

I appreciated the Courage and Wisdom of the YouTube presenter who put out a short, but thought-provoking video concerning the 2016 Super Bowl. (Anthony Gucciardi at http://naturalsociety.com/the-super-bowl-heres-what-you-wont-hear-on-tv/) In a scant one-minute-and-six-seconds he brought a little **reason** into the stuporous hype that engenders that yearly event. He challenged people to consider what great things could have been done for ourselves and our collective "Home" if all of that energy, money, time, thoughts, emotions, Voice Power, intentions, work, fuel, and every other form of "Energy" had been expended on other creative endeavors.

We learned in high school physics class that once "Energy" is generated it cannot be destroyed. …. Its **form** can be "changed", but the "Energy" itself can not be destroyed. So, that means that all of the "Energy" that was created around that particular sporting event **still exists,** and, by the laws of physics, **still has to be some where, doing some thing**. Hmmmmmm! If that **is** the case, then how **DO** we harness all that "Energy" for the good of mankind?

What intrigues me is that all of that newly created "Energy" was generated by the combined willful efforts **of the people!** It wasn't some engineered mechanical dynamo grinding out "Energy" to meet a specific need for industry or commerce. It was generated **by something within Us bipedal Hu-mans** that Our YouTube Friend is suggesting is powerful enough to make some much needed changes in our sandbox! **DoubleHmmmmm!**

Can it really be that simple? Are We, the People, **literally** individual Power Stations, Who can deliberately connect to, generate, and disseminate **"ENERGY"** by an act of Our conscious Will? ...? WOAH!!! If **that** really is the case, then perhaps we should take a new and different look at Ourselves! If We could truly get our minds around **that thought** we would live **differently!**

We would begin to be very careful how We **allowed** that creative volcano on the inside of Us to erupt!

We would begin to seek Wisdom before We opened its "vents" (which are Our thoughts, words, actions, intentions, and emotions), and allowed it to spew out in wasteful directions!

We would begin to see Ourselves as the **"Greatness"** that We really **ARE!**

We would begin to see Ourselves as being **Valuable** and **Important** parts of the "Hu-man dynamo" that, if Our theory is correct, could design, create, power, and enjoy **A Wonderful New World that is Beauteous To Behold!** Out of the **"Greatness"** that always travels with Us **We could create a world that We would all love to inhabit!**

It's all there, ..., **On the INSIDE of Us!** It's been building up pressure for eons, and **it is bursting at the seams!** It is an unstoppable **force** that is wanting to flow out of Our dreams and imaginings into the forms that Our commands create for them!

Wow! And here we were told, "It's just a "game". And, We were told how important it is to gather with family and friends, **as important as that is**, and eat party food, while rejoicing in someone else's wins and losses! **Triple Hmmmmm!**

Maybe Our YouTube Friend was right! We could have been celebrating accomplishments that We have not yet dared to dream, while eating luscious organically-grown superfoods that we didn't have to pay for or cook!

Yeah. I **DO** feel a poem coming on.

There's Greatness Within You

There's **Greatness**
    That's there
        On the Inside of **You**
           That the world
              Is awaiting
                To help make
                    ALL things New!!!

Its **The Radiance**
    Within **You**
        That Will blend
           With Great thought,
              To create
                A New Level
                  Of new things
                    As they ought!!

No more
    Lower Dimensions
        Of **Vibrations** so slow

            That they Can't
              Rise much higher
                Than Beneath
                  Your big toe!!

But,
> Dimensions of **Grandeur**
> And of **Beauty**
> And **Grace**

> That all
> Vibrate together,
> **Both** down here...
> And in Space, ...,

> To **Create**
> Something NEW,
> Of a **higher Vibration**,

> That will
> Lift Your Thoughts **HIGH**!! ...,
> And **Increase**
> Your Life's Station!

For,
Its **Thought Waves**
> That **seek,**

> As they
> Travel through Space,

> Other thought waves
> That **match**
> Their **Vibrations**
> And Place.

So,
    Whenever **You** wish
        To increase
            Your position,

        Just **Remember**,
            Your thoughts
                Seek like ones
                    Of condition.

We've been told
    That its "**Like**"
        That's attracted
           To "**Like**",

        So, its time
           that We send
                Lower thoughts
                    On a **HIKE**!!

Send them off,
    'Cause **they're <u>drawing</u>**
        OTHER "**Like**" thoughts
      To You.

(Could it be
    That **Your "thoughts"**
        Made Your own zoo?
           ...Its **TRUE**!!!)

Its NOT "OTHERS"
    That are attracting
        The mess that You're in,
            Its The "LEVEL Of Life"
                *That **You** sent*
                      To BEGIN!

Now,
    Its obvious
        HOW
            You can
                Lift Yourself UP!!

      Just be sure
          *Its The **Positive** Cup*
              *That **You** sup!!*

                        Vanessa Conaway Pace
                    October 27, 2006, Seattle, Washington,

There's Greatness Within You

**This Is *Your*
Invitation
To Create!**

Dear Seeker of Those "Deeper Things",

There is **Ge-ni-us** lurking
    On the *inside* of **You**, ...,
        But, could it be
            That You are **shirking**
                In some things
                    That You **do?**

There is something
    Within You
        That We **all**
           Truly **need**. ...

        So, ..., if You'll
           Indulge Us
                And **act**
                    With all speed, ...,

Our world
    Will be **better**, ...,
        And **richer**, ...,
           It's true,
                If You'll **open**
                    The door
                        To that **Geyser**
                            In You!!!

Now Its YOUR Turn To Be "Creator"!
Put YOUR Thoughts Here, and Read Them Later!

So, **That** Is the Charge
    I have for You, ...,
        Tune Your Creative Mind,
            And make all things **new**.

What ever your penchant
    For Creative things,
        Just dust them all off,
            And see what that brings!!!

Now Its YOUR Turn To Be "Creator"!
Put YOUR Thoughts Here, and Read Them Later!

Now Its YOUR Turn To Be "Creator"!
Put YOUR Thoughts Here, and Read Them Later!

Now Its YOUR Turn To Be "Creator"!
Put YOUR Thoughts Here, and Read Them Later!

Epilogue

www.pacepublishing.com

Epilogue

Now that We've finished
Our time
In this space,
Let Us think
On the projects
That We've
Put in place,

And the things
*That We've **learned***
As We've shared
This milieu,
*And the **plans***
That We're making,
And the things
*That We'll **do***

To enhance
Our Own lives,
*And **GROW***
All that We can,
And to somehow fit in
*To **The Great Plan***
*Of **Man***

That will soon
*Turn Our journey **OUT***
*From Our **Source**,*
*To an **INWARD** direction*
*That leads **Homeward**,*
Of course!

But now,
    In the interim time
        When we're **HERE,**
            We will use our time
                Wisely
                    With **thoughts**
                        That are **clear**

About **how**
    We would like
        Things
            To turn out to be
                In the orbit
                    Earth holds
                        In Our **great**
                            Galaxy.

Just imagine
    How happy
        Our life **here**
            Could be
                If We'd **all**
                    Work together
                        Like **One**
                            Family

That unites
    In **"Our Purpose",**
        And ignites
            All our rockets
                To give a great **Thrust**
                    To the dreams
                        In our pockets!

We'd have
    "Peaceful"
        For breakfast,
            And **"Joyful"**
                For lunch,
                    And for dinner
                        We'd have
                        A **Delirious** bunch

Of **The Happiest People**
    This Earth's
        Ever seen,
            'Cause **together**
                They'd **tuned up**
                      Earth's flying machine

So She's checked out
    To **fly**
        At some **loftier levels**
            And can leave
                Far behind
                    All those
                        Low Level Devils

Who have
    Pulled Us all **down**
        To a **heavier** place,
            And **that**
                Held Us back
                    From Ascension
                      In Space.

But We "**Happiest People**"
　　Have found out
　　　　THE SYSTEM
　　　　　　That helps Us
　　　　　　　　Get through
　　　　　　　　　　All the places
　　　　　　　　　　　　We've missed 'em!

And **together**
　　We'll journey
　　　　To a **spacious**
　　　　　　Dimension,
　　　　　　　　That is filled
　　　　　　　　　　With a **Grandeur**
　　　　　　　　　　　　That **absorbs**
　　　　　　　　　　　　　　Our attention

To things
　　Far above:....:
　　　　That We thought
　　　　　　We'd forgotten
　　　　　　　　While We slogged it out here
　　　　　　　　　　Amongst things
　　　　　　　　　　　　Misbegotten.

But, **Oh!** ...! It is **worth**
　　All the **time**,
　　　　And the **effort t**hat's needed
　　　　　　To get to
　　　　　　　　That place
　　　　　　　　　　Without being
　　　　　　　　　　　　Impeded!!

Sooooo, Just
    Roll up your sleeves
        And put your feet
           On the floor,...,
              ..., **Sing** and **Dance**
                  Your **Own** songs
                      More than ever
                        Before.

YES! We have shared much
    Together, ...,
        And there **Will be more**
           As we all
              Gather in
                  To enjoy
                      Volume 4!!!

www.pacepublishing.com

Epilogue

> ***This Is** Your*
> ***Invitation***
> ***To Create!***

Dear Seeker of Those "Deeper Things",

Remember, **Your part**
    In this planning
        And scheming
            Is to **bring to the fore**
            All that **You**
                Have been dreaming,

With the **daring**
    Of **"Pioneers"**
        Out on a mission
            To establish
                Our part
                    In this Hu-man
                      Condition!

You're a Creative part
    Of Our Earth's
        Chromoscope; ...;
            So, just **let**
                Your Light shine
                In Our
                      "Kaleidoscope"!

Now Its YOUR Turn To Be "Creator"!
Put YOUR Thoughts Here, and Read Them Later!

*Remember **You are part**
   In the **Great Plan**
      We are living,
         And get out your projects,
            And start
               Your own giving!!!*

Now Its YOUR Turn To Be "Creator"!
Put YOUR Thoughts Here, and Read Them Later!

Now Its YOUR Turn To Be "Creator"!
Put YOUR Thoughts Here, and Read Them Later!

Now Its YOUR Turn To Be "Creator"!
Put YOUR Thoughts Here, and Read Them Later!

Reading List

www.pacepublishing.com

Interesting Books To Reflect Upon: Volume 3

TITLE	AUTHOR	PUBLISHER	LOCATION
Beethoven's Nine Symphonies Correlated with the Nine Spiritual Mysteries	Corinne Heline	J. F. Rowny Press	Santa Barbara, CA
Elements of Acoustic Phonetics	Peter Ladefoged	The University of Chicago Press	Chicago, IL 60637
How Music Works: The Science and Psychology of Beautiful Sounds, from Beethoven to the Beetles and Beyond	John Powell	Little, Brown and Company, Hatchette Book Group	237 Park Avenue, New York, NY 10017
Molecules of Emotion: The Science Behind Mind-Body Medicine	Candace B. Pert, Ph.D.	Scribner	1230 Avenue of the Americas, New York, NY 10020
Nada Brahma: The World Is Sound: Music and The Landscape of Consciousness	Joachim-Ernst Berendt	Destiny Books	One Park Street, Rochester, VT 05767

Title	Author	Publisher	Address
Natural Brilliance: Overcome any challenge...at will	Paul R. Scheele	Learning Strategies Corporation	2000 Plymouth Road, Minnetonka, MN 553-5
Parallel Universes: The Search for Other Worlds	Fred Alan Wolf	Touchstone	1230 Avenue of the Americas, New York, NY 10020
Seven Mansions of Color	Alex Jones	DeVorss & Company	P.O. Box 550, Marina del Rey, CA 90294
Somatics: Reawakening the Mind's Control of Movement, Flexibility, and Health	Thomas Hanna	Addison-Wesley Publishing Company, Inc.	Reading, Massachusetts
The Brotherhood of Angels and of Men	Geoffrey Hodson	Ariel Press	88 Northgate Station Drive, #106, Marble Hill, GA 30148
The DNA Field and the Law of Resonance: Creating Reality through Conscious Thought	Pierre Franckh: Translated by Aida Sefic Williams	Destiny Books	One Park Street, Rochester, VT 05767

The Fairy Kingdom	Geoffrey Hodson	The Book Tree	P. O. Box 16476, San Diego, CA 92176
The Healing Code: 6 Minutes to Heal the Source of Your Health, Success, or Relationship Issue	Alexander Loyd, Ph. D., N.Md.	Grand Central Life & Style Hachette Book Group	237 Park Avenue, New York, NY 10017
The Language of Positive Thinking	A Blue Mountain Arts Collection	Blue Mountain Press SPS Studios, Inc.	P.O. Box 4549, Boulder, CO 80306
The Magic of Thinking BIG: Acquire the Secrets of Success....Achieve Everything You've Always Wanted	David J. Schwartz, Ph.D.	A Fireside Book Simon & Schuster	1230 Avenue of the Americas, New York, NY 10020
The Magical Path: Creating the Life of Your Dreams and a World That Works for All	Marc Allen	New World Library	14 Pamaron Way, Novato, CA 94949
The Personal Aura	Dora van Gelder Kunz	Quest Books The Theosophical Publishing House	P. O. Box 270, Wheaton, IL 60189
The Power of Sound: How To Be Healthy and	Joshua Leeds	Healing Arts Press	One Park Street, Rochester, VT

Productive Using Music and Sound		05767
The Spontaneous Healing of Belief: Shattering the Paradigm of False Limits	Gregg Braden	Hay House, Inc.	P. O. Box 5700, Carlsbad, CA 92018
The Vortex: Where the Law of Attraction Assembles All Cooperative Relationships	Esther and Jerry Hicks	Hay House, Inc.	P.O. Box 5100, Carlsbad, CA 92018
The Writing Diet: Write Yourself Right-Size	Julia Cameron	Jeremy P. Tarcher/Penguin	375 Hudson Street, New York, NY 10014
TNT: The Power Within You: How To Release The Forces Inside You & Get What You Want	Claude M. Bristol and Harold Sherman	A Fireside Book Simon & Schuster	1230 Avenue of the Americas, New York, NY 10020
Toning: The Creative and Healing Power of the Voice	Laurel Elizabeth Keyes with Don Campbell	DeVorss Publications	P.O. Box 1389, Camarillo, CA 93011
Unified System of Knowledge	Grigori Grabovoi	Trade Paper	Available at www.createspace.com

Request for Reader's Review

There's a "Poet"
    That's living
        On the inside
           Of YOU!!!

And Its speaking
    For The One
        That lives in Me
           TOO!

Hoping You
    Have enjoyed
        All these Books
           Through and through,

And that You'd
    Be so kind
        As to write
           A Review!!!

And to post it
    To Amazon's

        Page for this Book
           So that others
                Will know
                      To give THIS BOOK
                          A LOOK!!!

And maybe
    You'll send it
        To this "Poet"
            TOO!

So I can say
    "Thank You"
        For seeing that
            Through!!!

        This Poet,
      and The Poetry Muses,
    and all the new Readers
who are searching for this material
       will Thank You!!!

For
    Concerts that make
        You Laugh and Cry,

    Creative products
        That You'll want to buy,

    Poetry that makes
        You see new things,

    And Wisdom on Voice
        That'll help You Sing!

Contact Vanessa Pace at
    www.pacepublishing.com
    Post Office Box 2187, Lynnwood, WA 98036

Pace Publishing
Post Office Box 2187, Lynnwood, WA 98036
www.pacepublishing.com
E-Mail: poetry@pacepublishing.com

www.ingramcontent.com/pod-product-compliance
Lightning Source LLC
Chambersburg PA
CBHW030436300426
44112CB00009B/1021